DYNAMIC GUITAR

MORE TOOLS TO GO BEYOND STRUMMING

BY JEFFREY PEPPER RODGERS

Publisher: Lyzy Lusterman
Editor: Adam Perlmutter
Managing Editor: Stephanie Campos Dal Broi
Design and Production: Joey Lusterman

ISBN 978-1-936604-47-0

This book was produced by
String Letter Publishing, Inc.

330 Sir Francis Drake Boulevard, Suite C
San Anselmo CA 94960
(510) 215-0010; stringletter.com

DYNAMIC GUITAR

Introduction

AL NEVEU PHOTO

It's no wonder that acoustic guitar is the tool of choice for so many singer-songwriters and musicians of all kinds who accompany songs. Even with no other instruments, the acoustic guitar can deliver rich chords, lay down a powerful groove, fill out bass lines, and add hooks and riffs, and it can also be as quiet, delicate, and dreamy as you like. The guitar can be literally a band in a box—no bandmates (or electricity) required.

Getting this full-spectrum sound out of an acoustic guitar, with the versatility and range of a band, entails going beyond the go-to accompaniment technique of basic strumming. Strumming is essential and effective on the guitar, for sure, but it also has real limitations and can overpower the vocal and the groove. By varying the technique of both your fretting and picking hands—and often by playing *less*—you can do so much to make your guitar parts more dynamic and musically satisfying.

That's why I've created an extensive series of lessons on accompaniment for *Acoustic Guitar* magazine: to give you an array of tools for making chord progressions more distinctive, deepening grooves, and getting outside the box of strumming block chords.

My book/video guide *Beyond Strumming* offers 20 lessons, from the fundamentals of strong accompaniment to more advanced techniques like cross picking, hybrid picking, and alternate tunings. Now comes *Dynamic Guitar*, which shares six more vital tools for making the most of your guitar as an accompaniment instrument.

In these lessons, you'll learn how to build dynamics in an arrangement, how to play bass lines on guitar, and how to expand your chord vocabulary with slash chords and cluster chords. Plus you'll discover the possibilities of double-dropped-D tuning and the three-string partial capo—an amazing tool that allows you to create alternate tuning–like sounds without actually retuning. Along the way I share all sorts of examples inspired by classic songs, so you can hear and see how these tools work in actual music.

I hope you'll find many ideas here you can apply to your own arrangements—and maybe they'll spark your songwriting, too. Happy playing!

—Jeffrey Pepper Rodgers

Video Lessons

Each chapter includes an accompanying video lesson with Jeffrey Pepper Rodgers.

Go to **store.AcousticGuitar.com/DGVIDEO** to download your videos.

Notation Guide

Music is a language and, like many languages, has a written form. In order to be literate, one must become familiar with what each character and symbol represent.

Guitarists use several types of notation, including standard notation, tablature, and chord diagrams. Standard notation is a universal system in Western music. Becoming competent with standard notation will allow you to share and play music with almost any other instrument. Tablature is a notation system exclusively for stringed instruments with frets—like guitar and ukulele—that shows you what strings and frets to play to achieve the desired pitches. Chord diagrams use a graphic representation of the fretboard to show chord shapes on fretted instruments. Here's a primer on how to read these types of notation.

STANDARD NOTATION

Standard notation is written on a five-line staff. Notes are written in alphabetical order from A to G. Every time you pass a G note, the sequence of notes repeats, starting with A.

The duration of a note is depicted by note head, stem, and flag. Though the number of beats each note represents will vary depending on the meter, the relations between note durations remain the same: a whole note (𝅝) is double the length of a half note (𝅗𝅥). A half note is double the length of a quarter note (♩). A quarter note is double the length of an eighth note (♪). An eighth note is double the length of a sixteenth note (𝅘𝅥𝅯). And so on. You'll notice each time a flag gets added, the note duration halves.

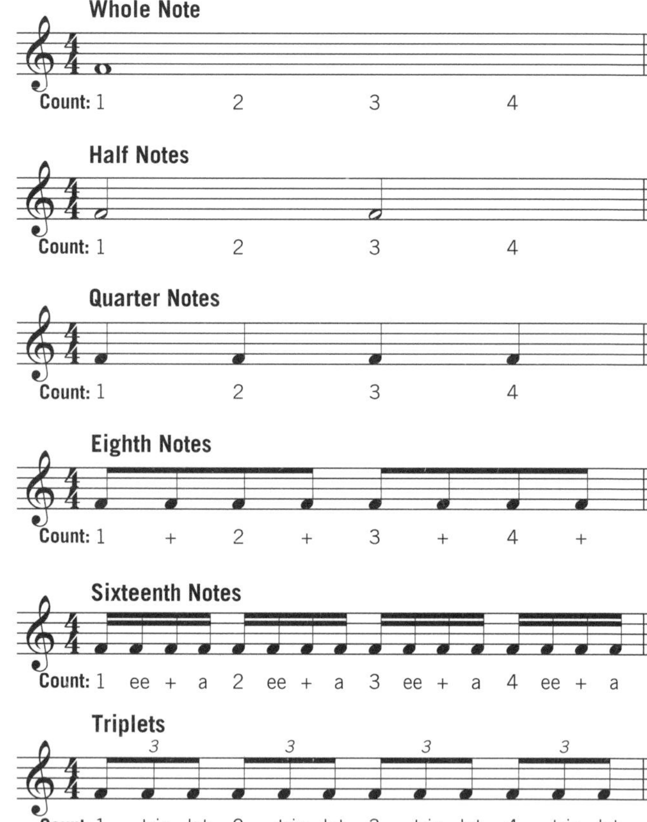

The numbers that follow the clef (4/4, 3/4, 6/8, etc.) or **C** shown at the beginning of a piece of music denote the time signature. The top number tells you how many beats are in each measure, and the bottom number indicates the rhythmic value of each beat (4 equals a quarter note, 8 equals an eighth note, 16 equals a sixteenth note, and 2 equals a half note).

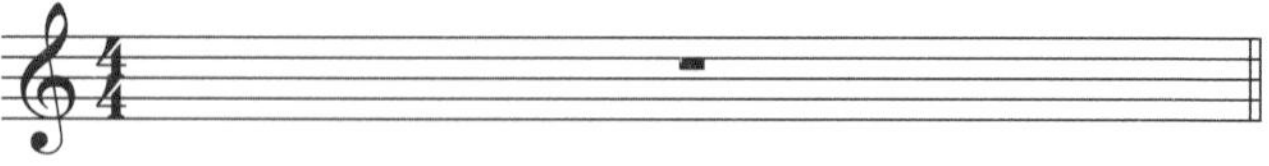

The most common time signature is 4/4, which signifies four quarter notes per measure and is sometimes designated with the symbol **C** (for common time). The symbol **¢** stands for cut time (2/2).

TABLATURE

In tablature, the six horizontal lines represent the six strings of the guitar, low to high, as on the guitar. The numbers refer to fret numbers on the indicated string.

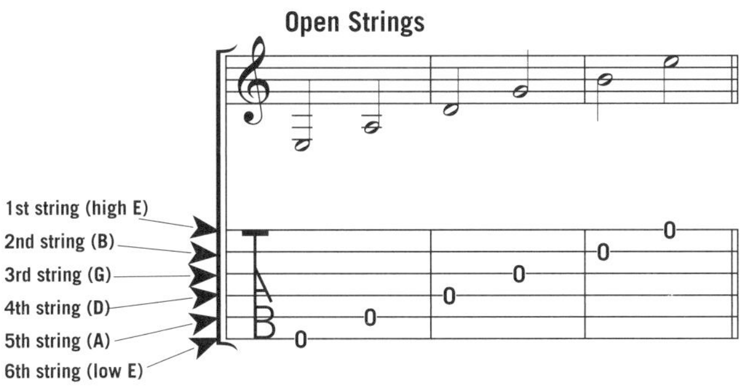

FINGERINGS

Fingerings are indicated with small numbers and letters in the notation. Fretting-hand fingering is expressed as 1 for the index finger, 2 the middle, 3 the ring, 4 the pinky, and *T* the thumb. Picking-hand fingering is conveyed by *i* for the index finger, *m* the middle, *a* the ring, *c* the pinky, and *p* the thumb.

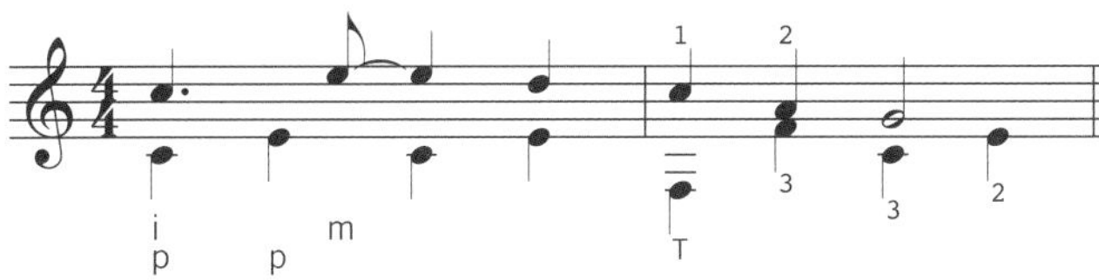

STRUMMING AND PICKING

In music played with a flatpick, downstrokes (toward the floor) and upstrokes (toward the ceiling) are shown as follows. Slashes in the notation and tablature indicate a strum through the previously played chord.

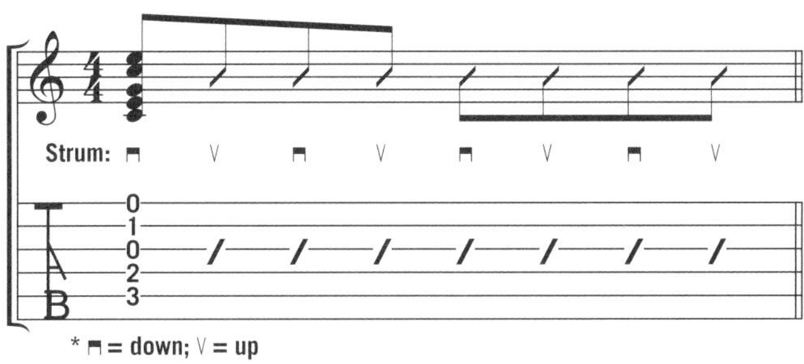

In music played with the pick-hand fingers, *split stems* are often used to highlight the division between thumb and fingers. With split stems, notes played by the thumb have stems pointing down, while notes played by the fingers have stems pointing up. If split stems are not used, pick-hand fingerings are usually present. Here is the same fingerpicking pattern shown with and without split stems. Clarity will inform which option is used.

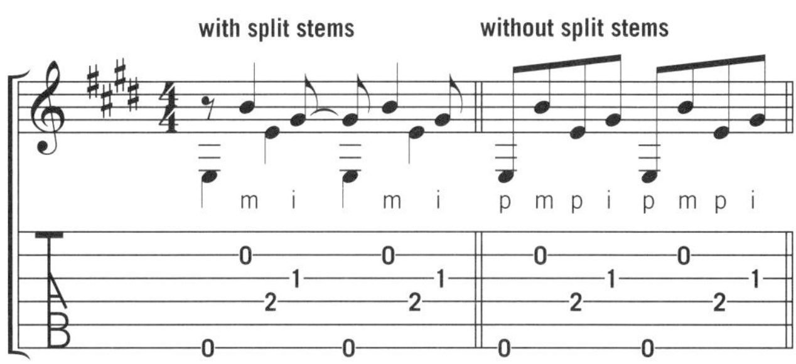

CHORD DIAGRAMS

Chord diagrams are a convenient way of depicting chord shapes. Frets are presented horizontally. The thick top line represents the nut. A fret number to the right of a diagram indicates a chord played higher up the neck (in this case the top horizontal line is thin and the fret number is designated). Strings are shown as vertical lines. The line on the far left represents the sixth (lowest) string, and the line on the far right represents the first (highest) string. Dots mark where the fingers go, and thick horizontal lines illustrate barres. Numbers above the diagram are fretting-hand finger numbers, as used in standard notation.

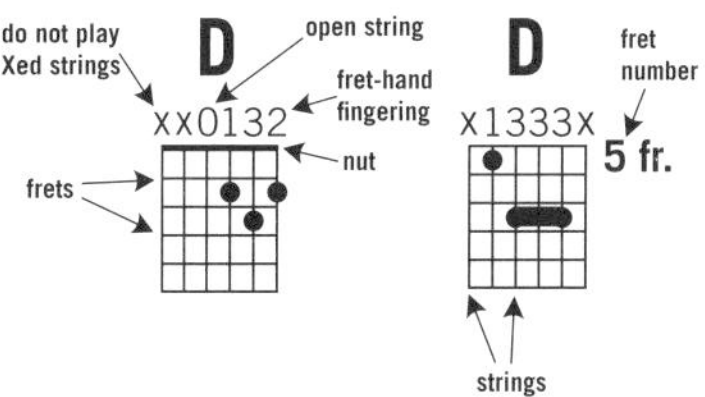

The given fingerings are only suggestions. They are generally what would most typically be considered standard. In context, however, musical passages may benefit from other fingerings for smoothest chord transitions. An X means a string that should be muted or not played; 0 indicates an open string.

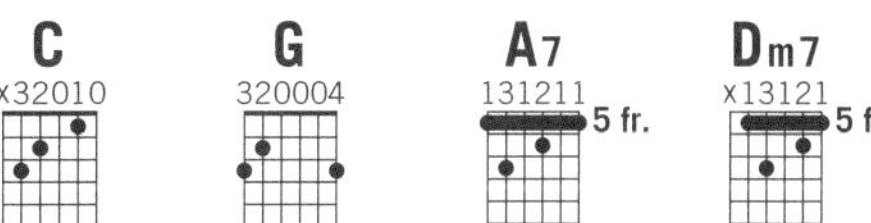

CAPOS

If a capo is used, a Roman numeral designates the fret where the capo should be placed. The standard notation and tablature is written as if the capo were the nut of the guitar. For instance, a tune capoed anywhere up the neck and played using key-of-G chord shapes and fingerings will be written in the key of G. Likewise, open strings held down by the capo are written as open strings.

TUNINGS

Alternate tunings are given from the lowest (sixth) string to the highest (first) string. D A D G B E is standard tuning with the bottom string dropped to D. Standard notation for songs in alternate tunings always reflects the actual pitches of the notes.

VOCAL TUNES

Vocal tunes are sometimes written with a fully tabbed-out introduction and a vocal melody with chord diagrams for the rest of the piece. The tab intro is usually your clue as to which strumming or fingerpicking pattern to use in the rest of the piece. The melody with lyrics underneath is that which is sung by the vocalist. Occasionally, smaller notes are written with the melody to indicate other instruments or the harmony part sung by another vocalist. These are not to be confused with cue notes, which are small notes that express variation in melodies when a section is repeated. Listen to a recording of the piece to get a feel for the guitar accompaniment and to hear the singing if you aren't skilled at reading vocal melodies.

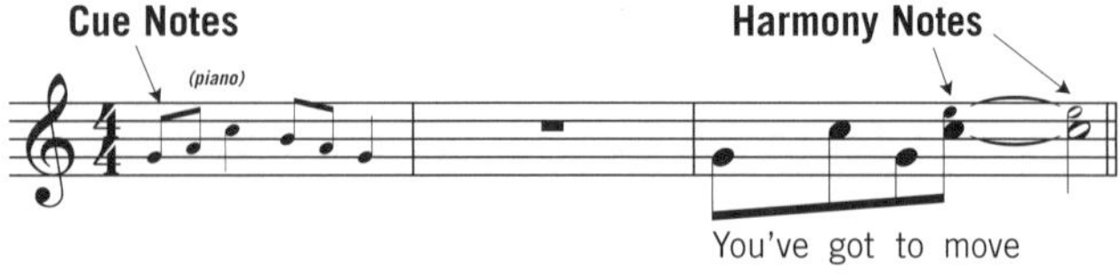

ARTICULATIONS

There are a number of ways you can articulate a note on the guitar. Notes connected with slurs (not to be confused with ties) in the tablature or standard notation are executed with either a hammer-on, pull-off, or slide. Lower notes slurred to higher notes are played as hammer-ons; higher notes slurred to lower notes are played as pull-offs.

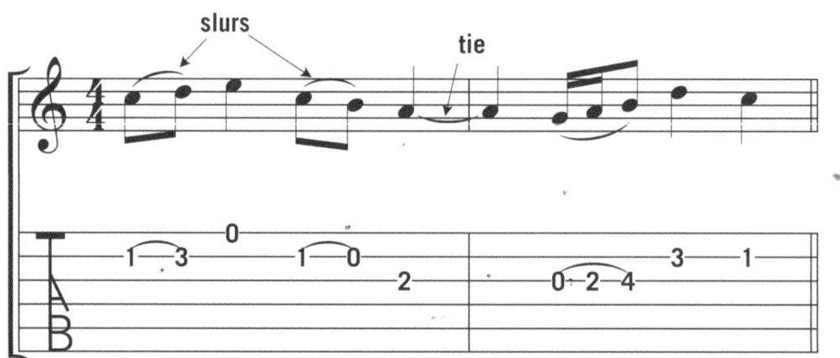

Slides are represented with dashes. A dash preceding a note is a slide into the note from an indefinite point in the direction of the slide; a dash following a note is a slide off the note to an indefinite point in the direction of the slide. For two slurred notes connected with a slide, pick the first note and then slide into the second.

Bends are denoted with upward arrows. Most bends have a specific destination pitch—the number above the bend symbol shows how much the bend raises the pitch: ¼ for a slight bend, ½ for a half step, 1 for a whole step.

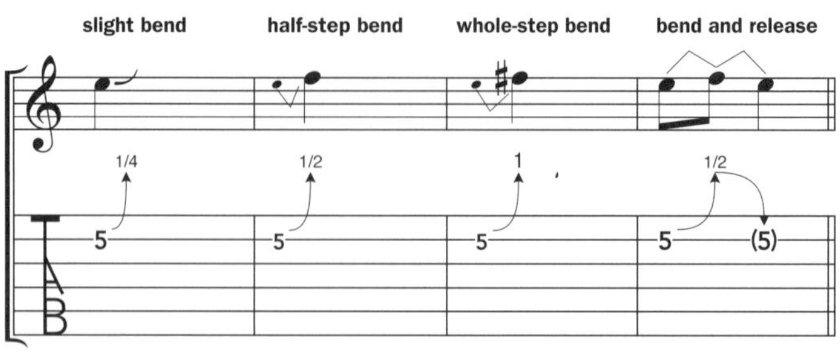

Grace notes are represented by small notes with a slash through the stem in standard notation and with small numbers in the tablature. A grace note is a quick musical ornament with no specific note value leading into a note, most commonly executed as a hammer-on, pull-off, or slide. In the first example below, pluck the note at the fifth fret on the beat, then quickly hammer onto the seventh fret. The second example is executed as a quick pull-off from the second fret to the open string. In the third example, both notes at the fifth fret are played simultaneously (even though it appears that the fourth string at the fifth fret is to be played by itself), then the fourth string, seventh fret is quickly hammered.

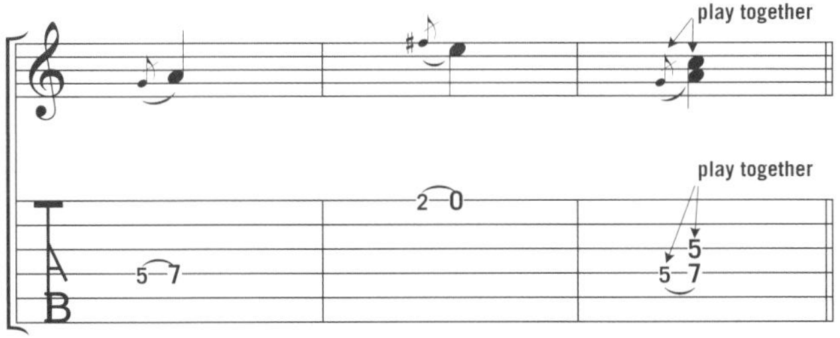

HARMONICS

Harmonics are expressed as diamond-shaped notes in the standard notation and a small dot next to the tablature numbers. Natural harmonics are indicated with the text "Harmonics" or "Harm." above the tablature. Harmonics articulated with the picking hand (often called artificial harmonics) include the text "R.H. Harmonics" or "R.H. Harm." above the tab. Picking-hand harmonics are executed by lightly touching the harmonic node (usually 12 frets above the open string or fretted note) with the picking hand index finger and plucking the string with the thumb, ring finger, or pick. For extended phrases played with picking-hand harmonics, the fretted notes are shown in the tab along with instructions to touch the harmonics 12 frets above the notes.

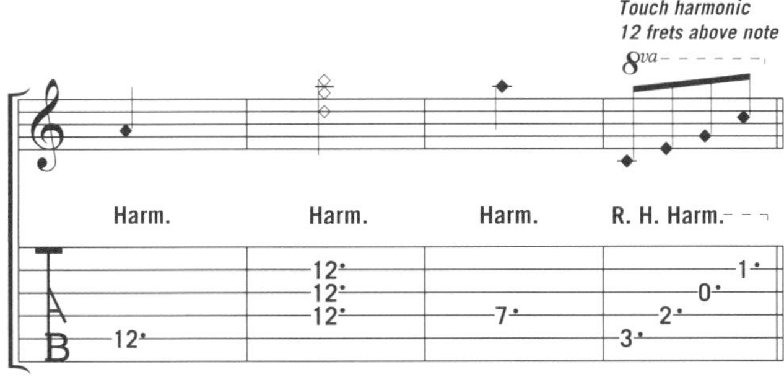

REPEATS

One of the most confusing parts of a musical score can be the navigation symbols, such as repeats, *D.S. al Coda*, *D.C. al Fine*, *To Coda*, etc. Repeat symbols are placed at the beginning and end of the passage to be repeated.

When you encounter a repeat sign, take note of the location of the begin repeat symbol (with the dots to the right of the lines), play until you reach the end repeat symbol (with the dots to the left of the lines). Then go back to the begin repeat sign, and play the section again.

If you find an end repeat only sign, go back to the beginning of the piece and repeat. The next time you get to the end repeat, continue to the next section of the piece unless there is text that specifically indicates to repeat additional times.

A section will often have a different ending after each repeat. The example below includes a first and a second ending. Play until you hit the repeat symbol, return to the begin repeat symbol, and play until you reach the bracketed first ending. Then skip the measures under the bracket and jump immediately to the second ending, and then continue.

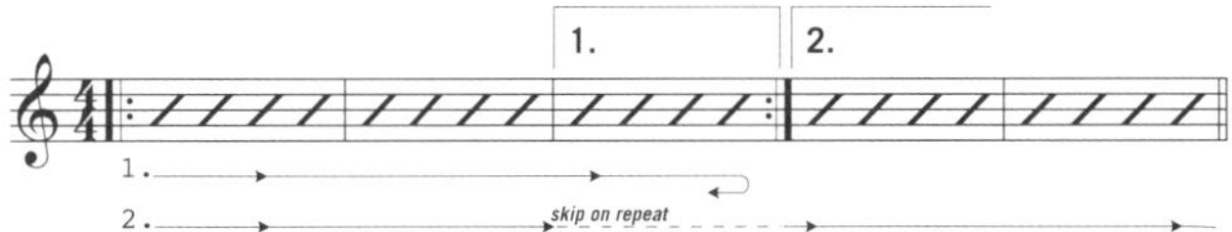

D.S. stands for *dal segno* or "from the sign." When you encounter this indication, advance immediately to the sign (𝄋). *D.S.* is usually accompanied by *al Fine* or *al Coda*. *Fine* indicates the end of a piece. A coda is a final passage near the end of a piece and is indicated with 𝄌. *D.S. al Coda* simply tells you to go back to the sign and continue on until you are instructed to move to the coda, indicated with *To Coda* 𝄌.

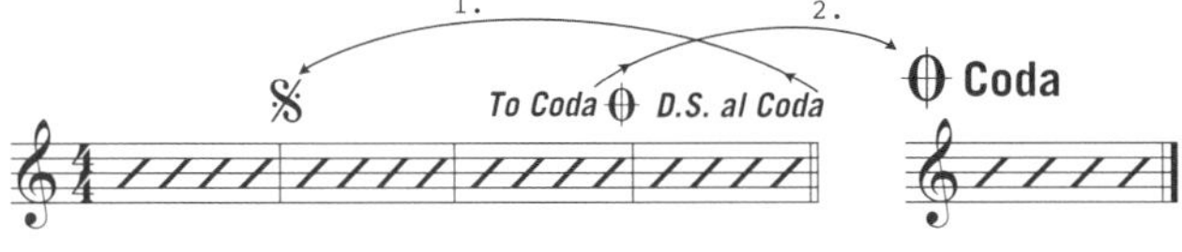

D.C. stands for *da capo* or "from the beginning." Jump to the top of the piece when you encounter this indication.

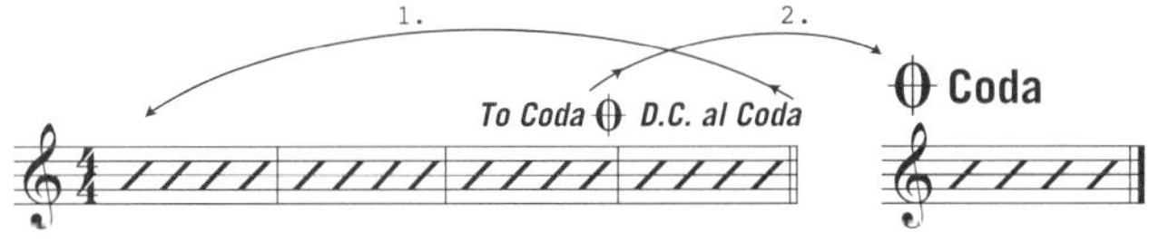

D.C. al Fine tells you to proceed to the beginning and continue until you encounter the *Fine* indicating the end of the piece (ignore the *Fine* the first time through).

DYNAMIC ARRANGING

Think of how a full band arrangement of a song might unfold. Perhaps a lone guitar and voice carry the first verse, and then bass and drums kick in; more instruments and voices join to lift up the chorus; the intensity continues to build, before releasing with a sparse final verse; and a big chorus takes it home. Like the song itself, the arrangement is its own little journey.

Even if you're accompanying a song with one guitar, you can create that same kind of journey on your instrument. The key is using dynamics, which come as much from what you leave out as what you play. If a band kicked off a song with every possible instrument playing full blast, there'd be nowhere to go but down in terms of volume and intensity, and the same is true of a single guitar part: If you start out playing all thick chords as hard as you can, you've boxed yourself in. By contrast—and the operative word here is *contrast*—a dynamic arrangement leaves space for the sound to get bigger or smaller, and evolve over the course of the song.

This lesson applies the dynamic arranging approach to the traditional song "Wayfaring Stranger." You'll practice creating varied textures and grooves over the same chord progression. I've based the examples on a performance of the song by my duo Pepper and Sassafras, with guitar and clarinet, that you can find at the end of this lesson's video.

Start Small

If you're not familiar with the haunting folk/gospel song "Wayfaring Stranger," check out the lead sheet. The song repeats the same 32-bar form throughout, using Em, Am, and B7 chords in the first section and adding C and G in the second section.

Example 1 (page 12) shows how the arrangement starts, up through the first verse. In the first three measures, play a short chord-melody intro using up-the-neck voicings of Am(add9) and B11 for a lush, jazzy sound. (In the duo version, the clarinet plays the intro melody and I just strum chords.) And then, in measure 3 (not counting the pickup measure), strip your part down to the bare minimum: a quarter-note pulse on the open sixth string. Add a little bit of palm muting if you wish—rest the side of your palm on the strings on top of the saddle or close to it on the fretboard side.

For the octave E in measure 3, fret the fifth string with your third finger. A lyric cue shows where the singing enters.

Opening the song like this, as if just the bassist were playing while the rest of the band sits out, creates an intimate feeling and invites an audience to lean in as the story begins: "I am a poor wayfaring stranger…"

When you go to Am in measure 9, fret the bass note on the sixth string. With your third finger at the seventh fret, your first finger is right in position for this.

Starting in measure 13, thicken your part slightly by adding some more octave E notes over the Em chord—as a bass player might do—and also a quick F# over the B7 chord in measure 18. Note that the octave riff falls between lines of lyrics, to give the vocal the full spotlight.

When the progression shifts to C, in measure 21, continue the accompaniment similarly: mostly quarter-note bass notes with occasional touches of other chord tones. On the B7 in measure 28, slide up the third string for an understated end to the phrase. Only in the next bar do you start adding a few soft strums, using open-string chord shapes up the neck for Em and Am(add9). For the B7 in measure 34, fret the third and fifth strings with a first-finger barre, and the fourth string with your third finger.

WAYFARING STRANGER

TRADITIONAL, ARRANGED BY JEFFREY PEPPER RODGERS

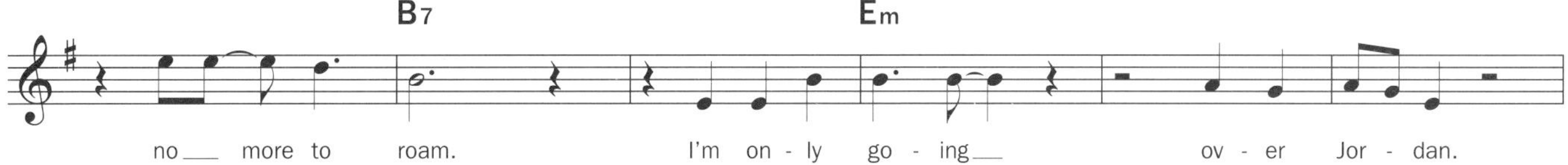

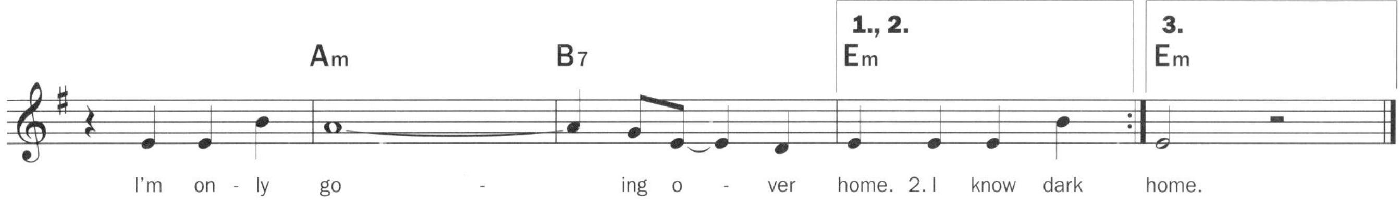

Em
2. I know dark clouds will gather 'round me
Am Em
I know my way is rough and steep

Yet beauteous fields lie just beyond me
Am B7 Em
Where souls redeemed their vigils keep
C G
I'm going there to see my mother
C B7
She said she'd meet me when I come
Em
I'm only going over Jordan
Am B7 Em
I'm only going over home

Em
3. I want to wear a crown of glory
Am Em
When I go home to that bright land

I want to shout salvation's story
Am B7 Em
In concert with the blood-washed band
C G
I'm going there to see my Savior
C B7
To sing His praise for evermore
Em
I'm only going over Jordan
Am B7 Em
I'm only going over home

Example 1

Freely
Moderately
Am(add9)
B11
Em
I am a
poor...
Am
Em
Am
B7
Em
I'm go - ing

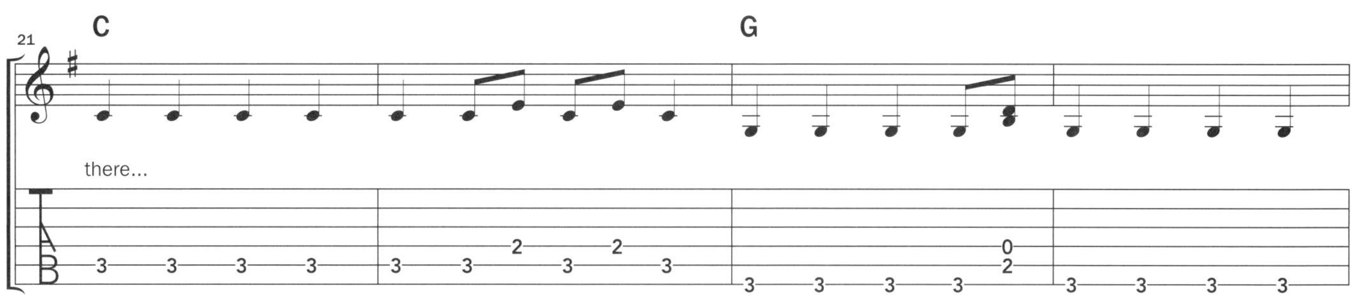
C
G
there...

C
B7

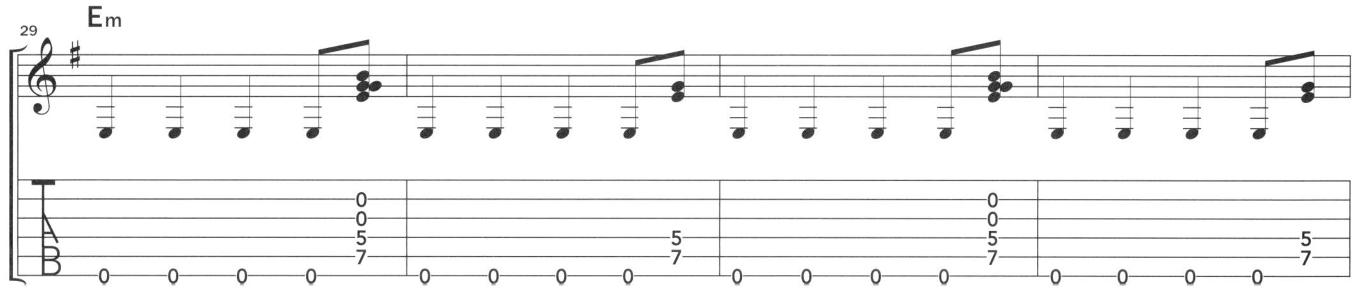
Em

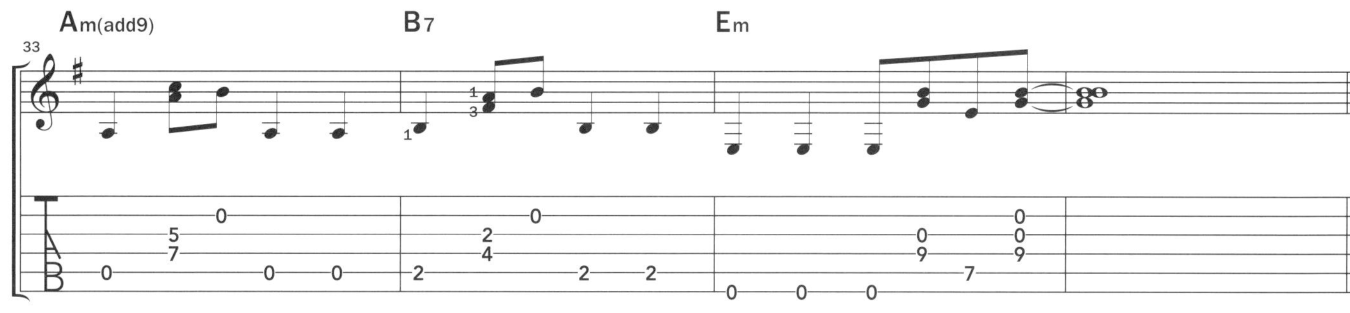
Am(add9)
B7
Em

Boost the Rhythm

When the second verse arrives, it's time to ramp up a bit. Bring in the drummer: switch to the more rocking groove in **Example 2,** using the octave and the seventh (the note D on Em and G on Am) and adding a percussive punch to the backbeats, as indicated with the accent marks (>). For the accents, come down on the bass strings a little harder with the pick, and with your palm as well for an extra thump. The edgier sound is right in sync with the lyrics: "I know dark clouds will gather 'round me."

When you arrive at the second section with the move to C, notice that you're now playing fuller chord voicings than in the first pass. The sound is slowly building as the story and song unfold.

For the last section of this verse, with the progression Em–Am–B7–Em (not shown in the notation), go back to playing something similar to the stripped-down pattern used at the end of Ex. 1, in measures 29 to 36.

Open into Full Chords

So where to go from here in the arrangement? In the duo performance, after the second verse comes an instrumental solo (more about that below). But for now, let's go to the final verse, when it's time to break away from the drone bass.

Example 3 shows the basic accompaniment pattern used in the third verse over Em and Am. On both chords, play a bass note on beat 1, a full strum on beat 2, and then either a quarter-note (down) or eighth-note (down-up) strum on beat 4. For Em, use the same fifth-position chord shape as before. Instead of an Am, use the more harmonically open Asus4, a voicing that fits the eerie mood well. At this point in the song, the guitar and vocals are at full intensity—in essence, the full band has kicked in, with a big backbeat.

Even when you're playing full chords like this, resist the urge to add constant up- and down-strums. Think like a drummer and focus on the backbeats.

Example 2

2.
Am
B7
Em
C
G
C
B7
Example 3
Em
Asus2
*Doubled B is eliminated in notation, for ease of reading.

Example 4 shows one way to play the Am–B7–Em changes in this climactic verse. For the B7, add in the open first string to make it a B7sus4.

Then, on the second half of the verse, start using an alternating bass, as shown in **Example 5**. Since you've played a monotone bass up to this point in the song, this change to alternating has a real impact—it gives the progression a whole different type of momentum. On the G chord, throw in a little single-note bass riff, too, for additional movement. Again, because of the restraint of the guitar part in earlier verses, these new developments make a dramatic contrast.

Go Home

After the song reaches its climax in verse three, the last piece of the arrangement is the closing line and tag: "I'm only going over Jordan" followed by three repetitions of "I'm only going over home." At this point, strip the guitar back down to a sparse pattern similar to what you played at the top, with the monotone bass and just a few light strums, as shown in **Example 6**.

Just for a subtle variation, the first four measures of Ex. 6 use a slightly different voicing of Em than elsewhere. Play this whole section softly, bringing listeners close again. In the last four measures, over the ritard, return to the chord shapes you started with: Am(add9) and B11, and then a final Em11. The arrangement is literally coming full circle, as the narrator sings of "going home."

When you're working on your own guitar arrangements, think about ways to create this kind of dramatic arc during a song. You don't necessarily have to start quietly and get louder, but work on varying the textures to differentiate the sections from each other and to create growth and change in the song. Take your cue from the lyrics, and think of the guitar as not just providing the rhythm but telling a story.

Add a Melodic Solo

One great way to enhance your guitar arrangements is to add an instrumental break or riffs based on the melody. With "Wayfaring Stranger" in the key of E minor, it's pretty straightforward to play the melody while keeping the rhythm and harmony going. Just be sure to hit the appropriate root bass note on the first beat when the chord changes, to establish the new chord. **Example 7** shows the first four bars to get you started. Try picking out the rest of the melody from here.

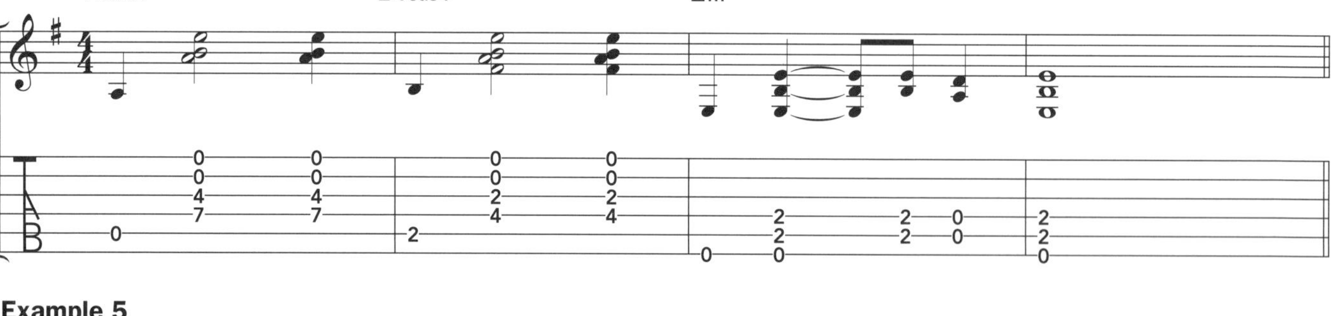

Example 5

Example 6
Em
Am(add9)
B7
1.
Em
2.
Em
rit.
Am(add9)
B11
Em11
Example 7
Em

SLASH CHORDS

Slash chords are an essential tool for adding variety to chord progressions and creating smoother movement from chord to chord. The slash refers literally to the chord symbol, as in G/B—usually spoken as "G slash B" or "G over B"—which simply means that you're playing a note other than the root on the bottom of the chord. This small change to a chord voicing can have a big impact on the sound of a progression, as we'll explore in this lesson.

We'll build a library of slash chord shapes through a series of examples based on the chord progression to "A Whiter Shade of Pale," Procul Harum's iconic song from 1967, with its Bach-inspired organ accompaniment. The song uses slash chords throughout to create powerful descending chord movement, and provides a useful platform for developing your slash chord vocabulary.

Slash Chord Basics

The simplest type of slash chord is an inversion—that is, a rearrangement of the notes in the chord.

A C major triad, for instance, has the notes C (root), E (third), and G (fifth); when they are stacked in that order, with C on the bottom, that's just called a C chord (or C major). Putting the fifth on the bottom, so the chord is spelled, say, G–C–E, creates the slash chord C/G. The fifth is a very common alternate bass note in any chord, so an inversion like this makes a subtle change in the harmony.

Another common slash chord voicing puts the third of the chord as the lowest note, as in C/E. Inversions with the third on the bottom sound less resolved than ones stacked on the fifth.

In addition to inversions, you'll encounter slash chords that have a bass note that's not in the basic triad, as in C/B or D/C. These sorts of slash chords are often transitional, creating bass movement leading to another chord; you might, for instance, play C to C/B to Am, with the bass descending in steps from C to B to A. You'll see that kind of movement throughout the examples below.

Descending in C

Now let's jump in and try some slash chords in an example based on the intro/interlude progression in "A Whiter Shade of Pale." The essence of the song is that chords change every two beats (and sometimes more often), and the bass line descends in steps almost nonstop; when the bass gets to the lower end of the register, it jumps up an octave and starts descending again. My fingerstyle guitar adaptation uses the same type of descending movement, and what makes that possible is—you guessed it—lots of slash chords.

First play the progression in C, the song's original key. In **Example 1,** you'll find a number of slash chord shapes with the fifth in the bass: Em/B, C/G, Am/E, F/C, and G7/D. The F/A and G7/B in measure 8 have the third in the bass. On the G/F in measure 5, the F♮—a note that's not in a G triad—moves the bass line toward the Em that follows.

Begin the example on a C and immediately start descending in the bass: To Em/B, Am, C/G, F, and Am/E. At that point, you've hit your lowest bass note in standard tuning, so jump up to the fourth string for Dm, and descend again from there: The bass notes go to C, G, F, and E, before looping back up to D on the G7/D.

For the main arpeggio pattern in these examples, pick the bass note with your thumb, followed by: index, middle/ring together, and index again.

Note that the chord sequence in measures 1–6 accounts for the bulk of "A Whiter Shade of Pale." In the verse (not shown), you play this six-bar sequence twice, and then once again to kick off the chorus.

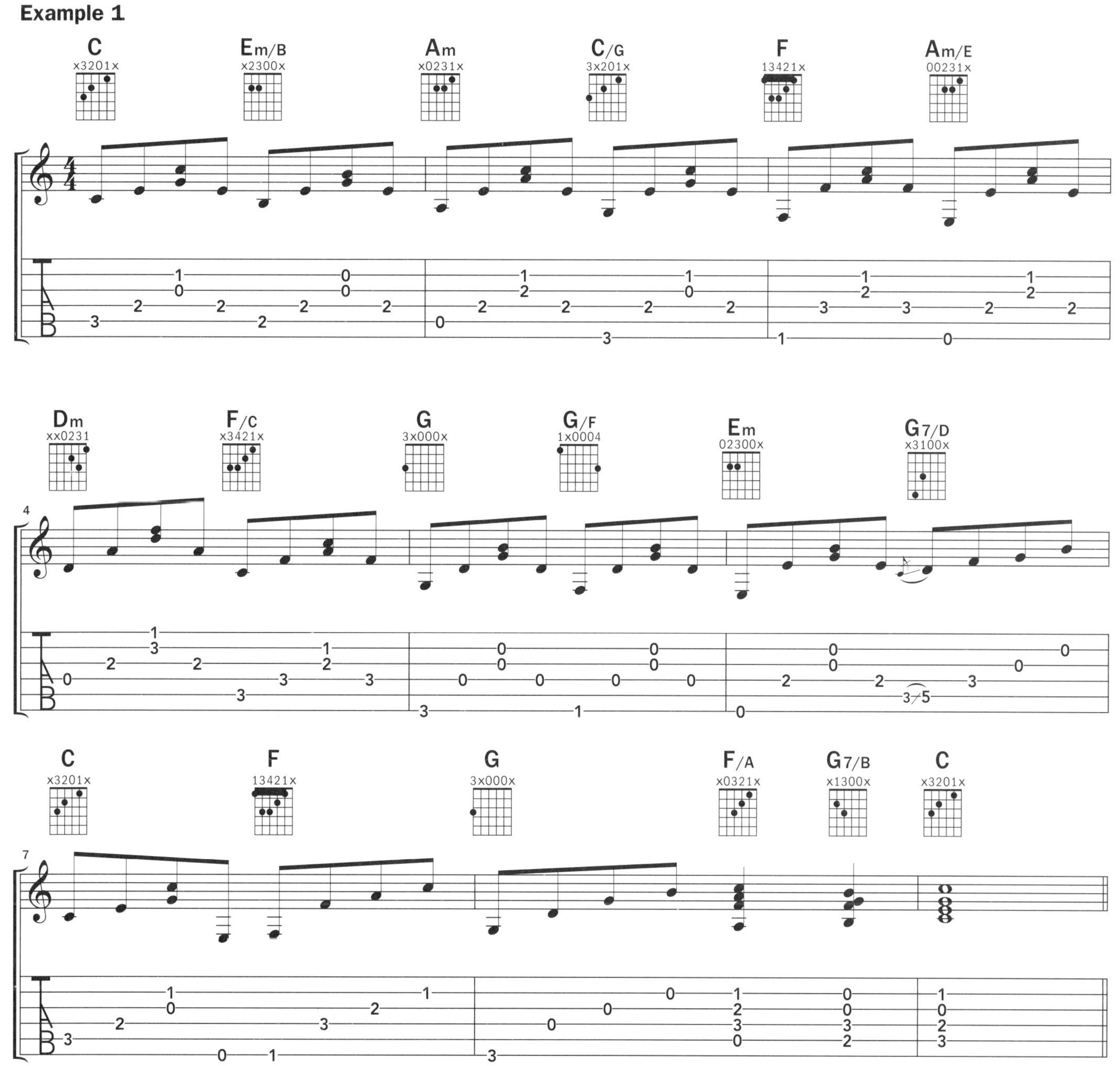

Keys of G and D

Once you've got this chord sequence under your fingers in the key of C, try it out in a few more keys. Through the following examples, the picking pattern is very similar to the one used in C, but these other keys employ some different slash chord shapes.

In **Example 2**, play the progression in the key of G, again using slash chords with the fifth in the bass (Bm/F♯, Em/B, C/G, D7/A), with the third in the bass (C/E, D7/F♯), and with a note outside the chord in the bass (D/C).

For the Bm/F♯ in measure 1, the shape could include a fifth-string B, but I've opted to leave it out so there's more separation between the notes on the sixth and fourth strings. The same is true for the C/G in measure 4, in which the fifth string is muted. In some musical contexts, you may want to mute or skip strings like this in a slash chord to put more emphasis on your alternate bass note.

In other chord shapes in this lesson, too, I've left out strings that could be included. The D7/F♯ in measure 8, for instance, could have an additional F♯ note on the

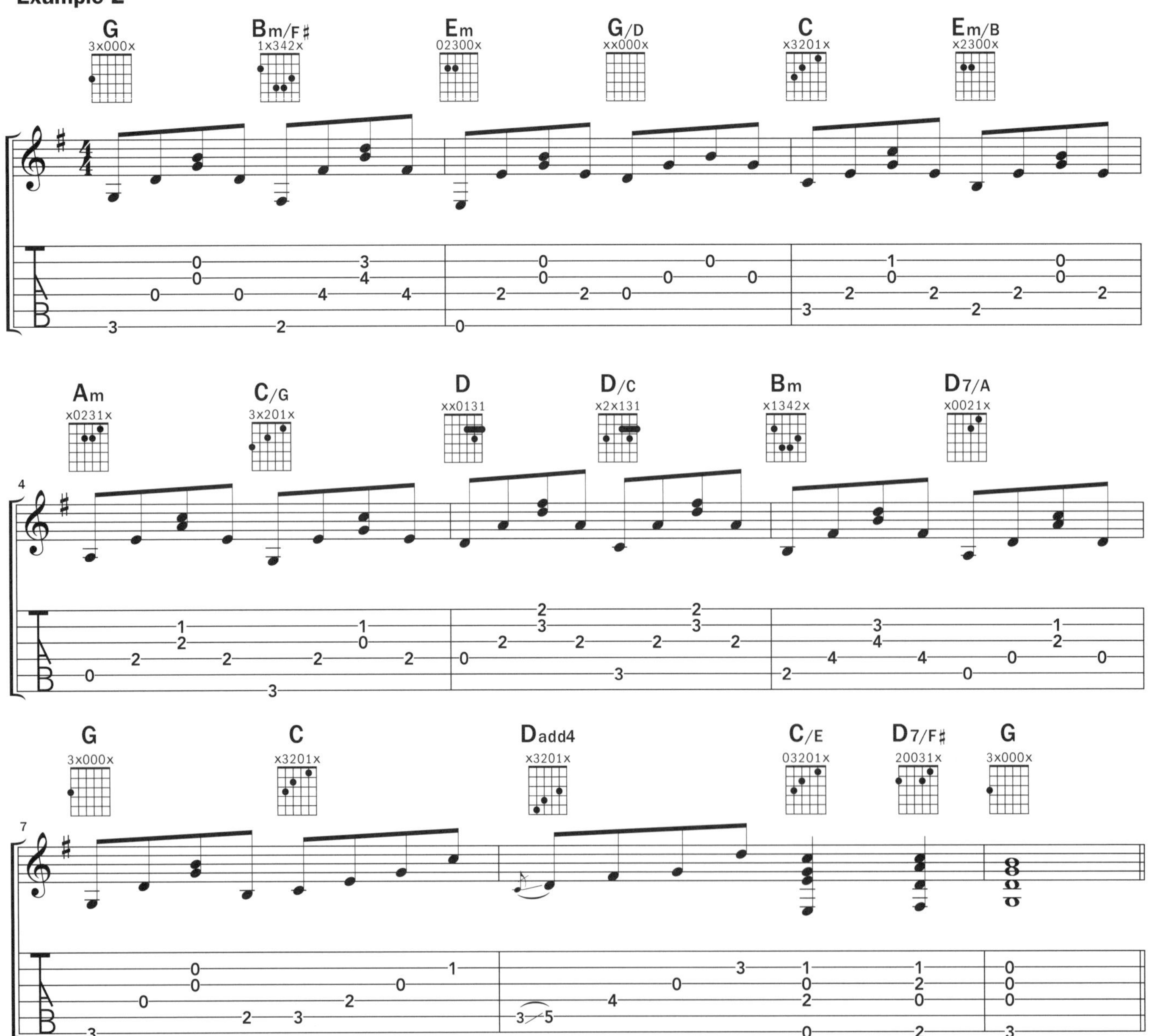

first string. I'm reducing this chord because I prefer its tighter sound—plus this fingering is a bit easier to play.

In measure 5, hold the D chord shape with an index finger barre and your ring finger so that you can easily add the middle finger on the fourth string for the D/C. In measure 8, slide the C shape up two frets for the Dadd4, and then play a C/E to D7/F♯ to G for a sweet, hymn-like closing cadence. The slash chord C/E, with the open sixth string, is surprisingly uncommon considering how easy it is to play, and it makes a nice transition to an F or, as in this example, a D/F♯.

In **Example 3**, play in the key of D. Start with a closed-position D at the second fret and descend in the bass to the open fourth string, then continue down to the sixth string E. For the A in measure 5, use a first-finger barre to set yourself up for the following A/G.

Keys of A, E, and F

Now play the same progression in three other keys to work through additional slash chord shapes and moves.

Playing this progression in the key of A, in **Example 4**, offers some nice options for extending the chord voicings with open strings. Play the A in fifth position in measure 1 for a smooth shift to the C♯m/G♯, and continue the descent to the A/E. In measure 6, leave the top two strings open for a lush C♯m7 and an E7/B up at the sixth and seventh frets.

Example 4

The key of E also presents opportunities to use more open strings. In **Example 5**, through the first four chords (E, G♯m/D♯, C♯m7, E5/B), let the open second string ring while the other voices descend.

In measure 5, hold the fourth fret barre with your ring finger through the B, B/A, and G♯m7. The B7/F♯ that follows is a handy all-around slash chord shape that is a staple of swing rhythm—and it's movable if you leave out the open second string.

Example 5

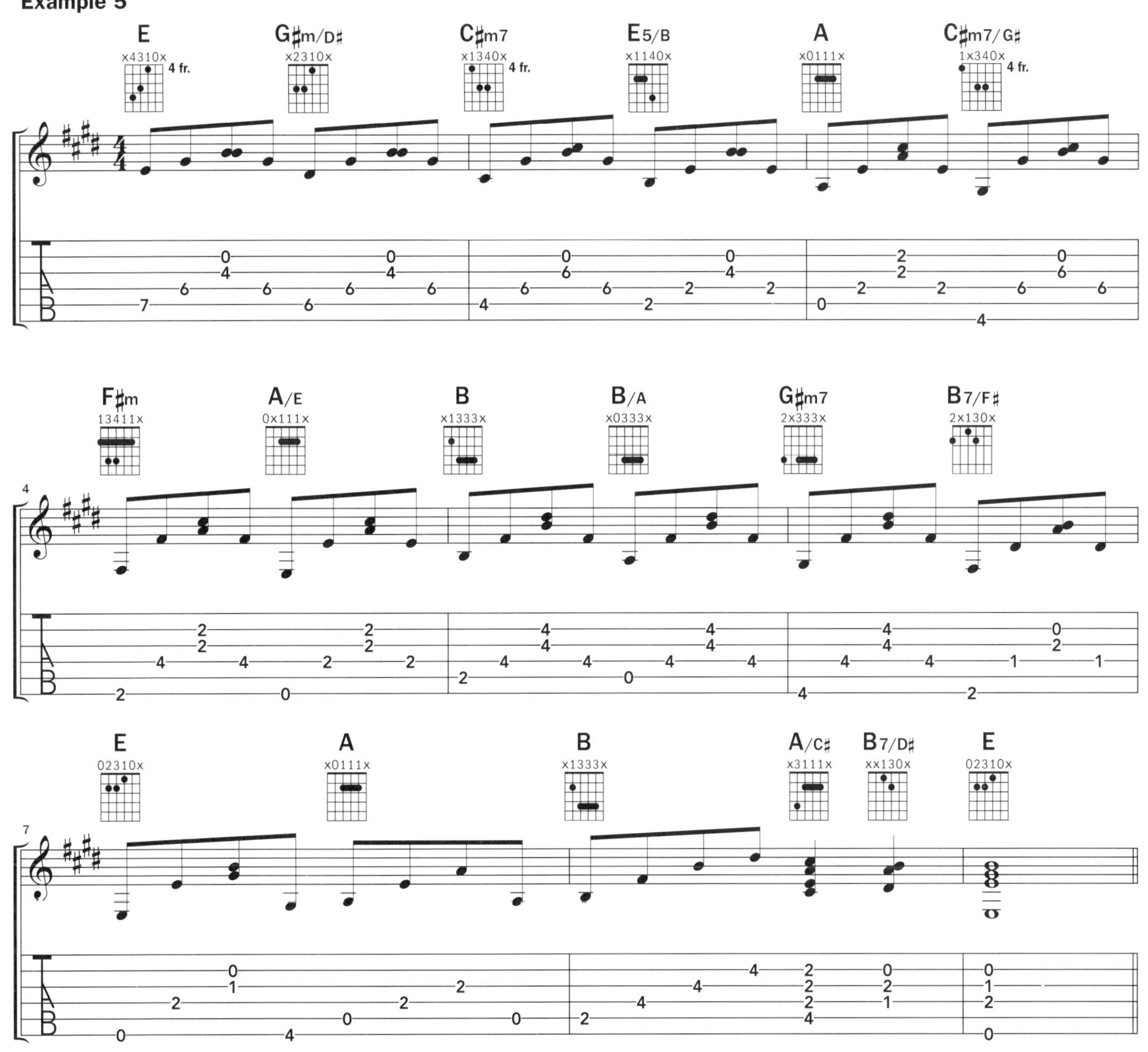

Finally, check out every guitarist's favorite key, F, in **Example 6**. You may be surprised by how nicely this progression falls in F, with a lot of open-position slash chords (Am/E, Dm/A, C7/G, and more).

Start with an F shape on the top four strings and descend an octave through the first four measures, down to an F on the sixth string. In measures 3 and 4, keep your fourth finger planted on string 2, fret 3, while you change from Dm/A to Gm to B♭/F.

In measures 5 and 6, play the third string open through the C to C/B♭ to Am7, creating a common tone as you move from chord to chord.

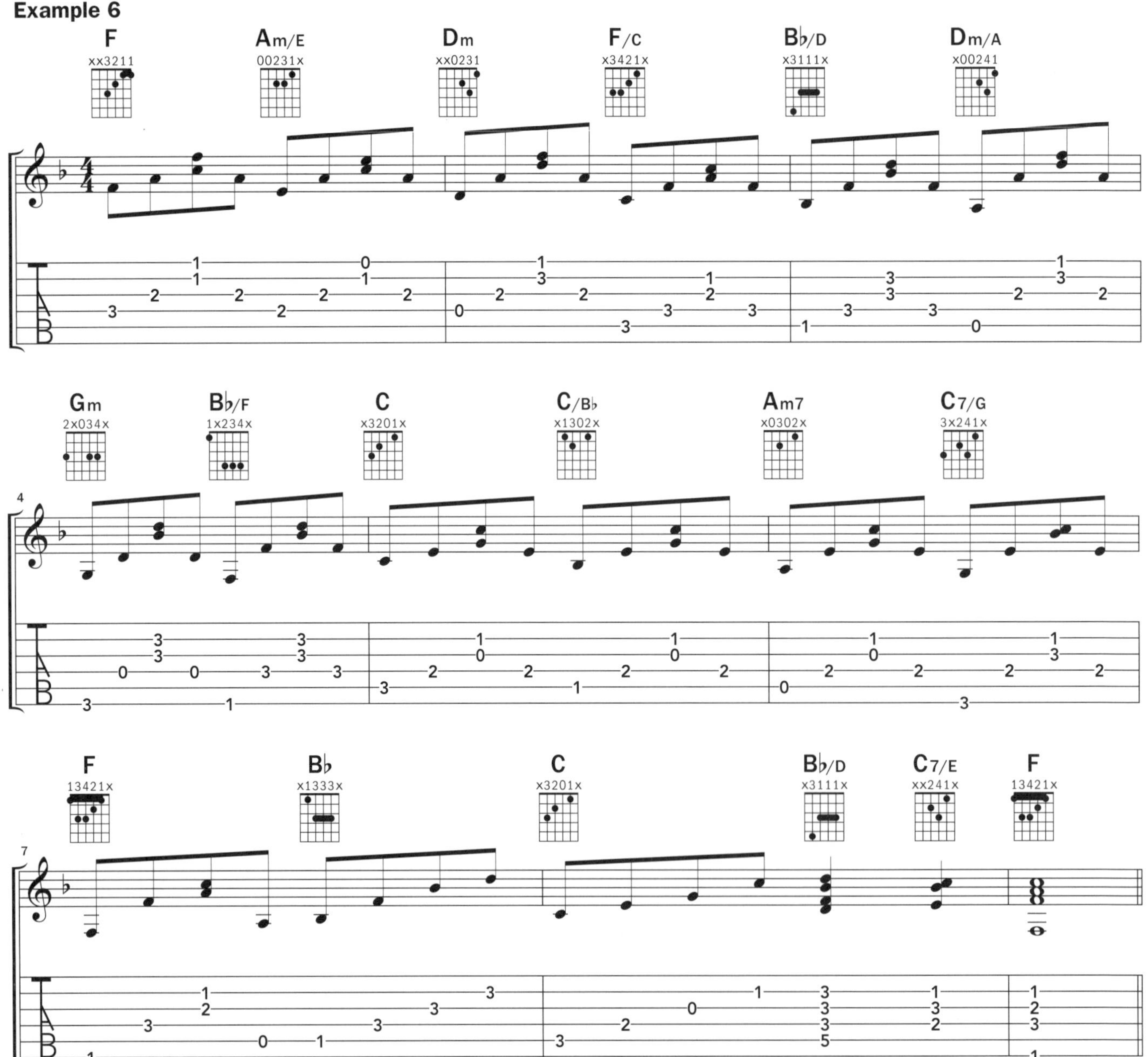

Moving Chords

Another good use of slash chords is to add movement to a progression. In **Example 7**—not based on "A Whiter Shade of Pale"—the basic harmony is D, Bm, G, A: one measure each, a classic I–vi–IV–V. I've split each measure in half to add a slash chord on beat 3 that moves the bass toward the next chord. The D/C♯ makes a nice transition to the Bm, for instance. Look for places like this where you can use slash chords to set up chord changes.

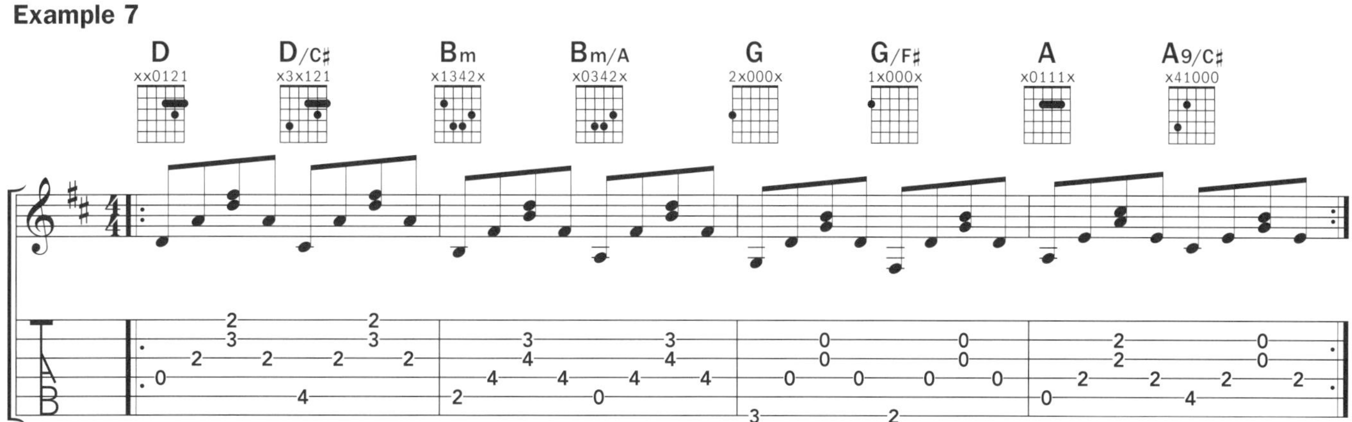

BILL EVANS PHOTO

An A9/C♯ works well as a connecting chord between A and D.

Arranging with Slash Chords

Now that you've tried out examples in six keys, you've covered quite a few shapes and combinations of slash chords. As you arrange other songs, try substituting slash chords in order to create a more connected sound in the progression, and to develop bass lines that move in smaller steps rather than jumping around. These subtleties in how you voice the chords will make your whole guitar part more mellifluous and satisfying.

PLAY BASS

You see it at just about every jam, whether in the living room or the festival parking lot: the wall of guitars. Almost everyone holds a flattop guitar, and when someone kicks off a song, the air fills with six-strings ringing out the same chords. Best case scenario, people listen to each other, hold down a solid rhythm, and don't drown out the singing or instrumental solos. Worst case—the cumulative sound is like a slow-motion train wreck with a familiar song playing in the background.

But hey, you play guitar, and that's the instrument you have at the jam. What to do? One approach is to figure out a part in a different register. If everyone's strumming open chords in the key of G, for instance, you could put a capo at the seventh fret and use key-of-C shapes instead. An even better idea might be to skip the chords entirely and simply play bass lines on your guitar.

Even if there is an actual bass player at the session—or in a band, for that matter—you can add a lot to the groove and feel of songs by working the low end on the guitar. When you are playing with just one other guitarist, too, focusing on bass lines can be a great way to enhance the sound without overlapping the other person's part.

In this lesson, you'll practice some techniques for playing bass on guitar, from alternating roots/fifths and bass runs to octaves and the walking bass, using the chord progressions from some perennial jam session favorites. In the video, I play the bass lines shown in the examples under a basic rhythm/chordal part.

Alternating Bass Style

If you use the classic boom-chick style on the guitar, you are essentially playing bass while covering chords as well—the boom is the bass and the chick is the strummed chord. So how about just taking out the chords and spotlighting the bass? That's what you'll do in **Example 1**.

The common chord progression of this example is used in the song that's been at the top of the jam session charts for a while now: "Wagon Wheel," by Old Crow Medicine Show and Bob Dylan. It's nothing fancy: I–V–vi–IV and then I–V–IV in the key of A (often played on guitar with G shapes and a capo at the second fret).

In the first eight bars of Ex. 1, you simply alternate between the root and the fifth for each chord. On the A chord, play A (root) and E (fifth); on the E chord, play E (root) and B (fifth); and so on. You can use a flatpick or your thumb, or alternate your index and middle fingers, as many bass players do. If you play with a pick, try muting the bass strings by resting your palm on the bridge to get a little more thump.

Although the notation mostly shows half notes, if you listen closely to bass players you'll notice that they often leave space between notes to create more rhythmic bounce. To get that sound, you'll need to cut notes short with muting. It's easier to mute fretted strings than open strings, so when playing bass you might opt for fretted notes, as in measures 7–8, where you grab D and A at the fifth fret even though you could use open strings.

In measures 9–16 of the example, take a second pass through the progression, this time with adding some short quarter-note bass runs for a little more movement. In "Wagon Wheel," you could play a part like this on the chorus and then go back to the straight alternating bass for the verses, to add contrast between sections.

Example 1

Play Octaves

In addition to roots and fifths, bass players use lots of octaves, so that's the focus of the next example, based on "The Weight," by the Band.

The verse, chorus, and interlude in **Example 2** use octaves throughout—on the sixth and fourth strings, and on the fifth and third strings. The song has a sweet syncopated feel that this bass part accentuates. If you're playing with people who are just strumming the chords, this bass line will make the music groove much more.

Through most of the verse and chorus, you play the octaves sequentially—the low note and then an octave up. But from measure 8 through the end of the interlude, play the octaves together; you can pick the individual strings fingerstyle or, if you're using a flatpick, mute the string in between. The octaves sound particularly good on the interlude that follows the chorus, with the descending line from G to C.

Notice the staccato marks (dots) in the verse notation—play these notes shorter than written.

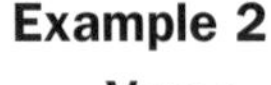

Example 2

Verse

Chorus

Interlude

JEFFREY PEPPER RODGERS PHOTO

Roots, Thirds, and Fifths

Next, practice a common bass pattern that uses the three notes of a basic triad: root, third, and fifth. To dial in the rhythm, count the eighth notes as 1-2-3, 1-2-3, 1-2, and play a bass note on each 1. It's an easygoing, relaxed feel—perfect for a song like Jimmy Buffett's "Margaritaville," the basis of the example.

For **Example 3**, first tune to dropped D. Since the progression is in D, you'll be able to make good use of that low D on the sixth string. I also use dropped D to play bass lines in other keys, like G or A—that extra bit of range makes a big difference.

"Margaritaville" sits on the same chords for a long time in the verse, so this moving bass line really helps to liven up the sound of static strumming. For most of the example, play a root–third–fifth pattern, with a few variations and some connecting bass runs, as in measure 16 (leading into the chorus).

Stay in position throughout the example, with the first, second, third, and fourth fingers covering the notes on frets 2, 3, 4, and 5, respectively.

Example 3

Dropped-D Tuning (D A D G B E)

Verse

D

A

D
Chorus
G
A
1., 2.
D
3.
D
A
G
A
D
G
A
D

Walking Bass

Finally, practice the walking bass—moving on nearly every beat. Put on your shades and think upright bass for the bass moves in **Example 4**, based on Van Morrison's "Moondance."

The first seven measures of the verse, in which the chords bounce back and forth between Am7 and Bm7, show a bunch of variations that you can mix and match to create your own line. In measure 8, walk up to the Dm and keep on going through measure 14. After the transitional Dm and E7 in measures 15 and 16, in the chorus the chord changes between Am to and Dm go twice as fast. Anticipate both chords by playing the roots an eighth note before the on beats. In measures 16 and 24, add a little heft to your E bass notes by doubling them at the octave.

Playing bass lines like this on guitar has benefits beyond the public service of making jam sessions sound better. It'll make your more conscious of your guitar's low end, which is very healthy even when you're playing chords too. And hey, when there's a call for an actual bass player for a jam, concert, or recording session, you're primed for the gig. Just carry your bass lines right over from your guitar. Those big fat basses are, after all, tuned the same as your bottom four strings.

Swing

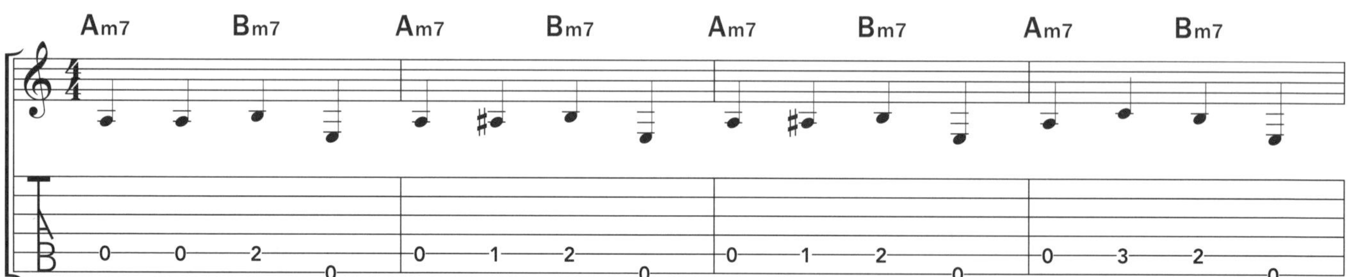

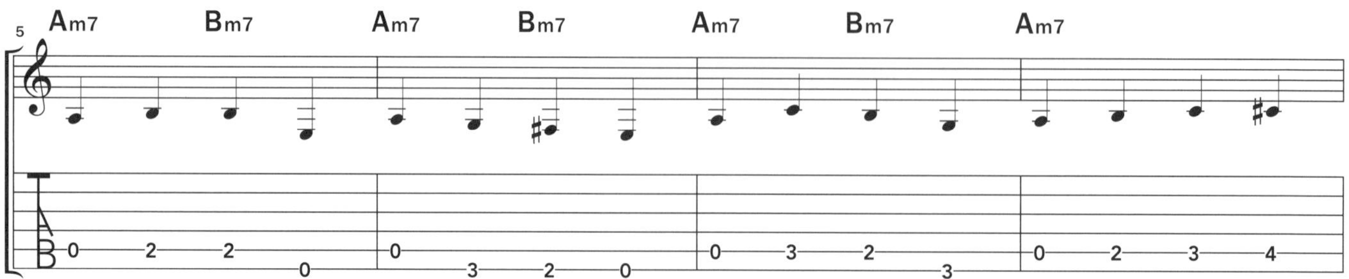

9
Dm
Am
Dm
Am

13
Dm
Am
Dm
E7

Chorus

17
Am
Dm
Am
Dm
Am
Dm
Am
Dm

21
Am
Dm
Am
Dm
Am
Dm
E7

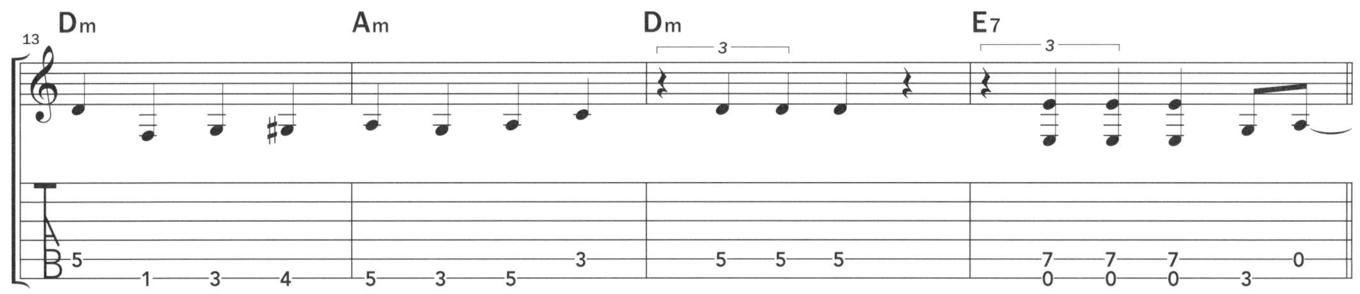

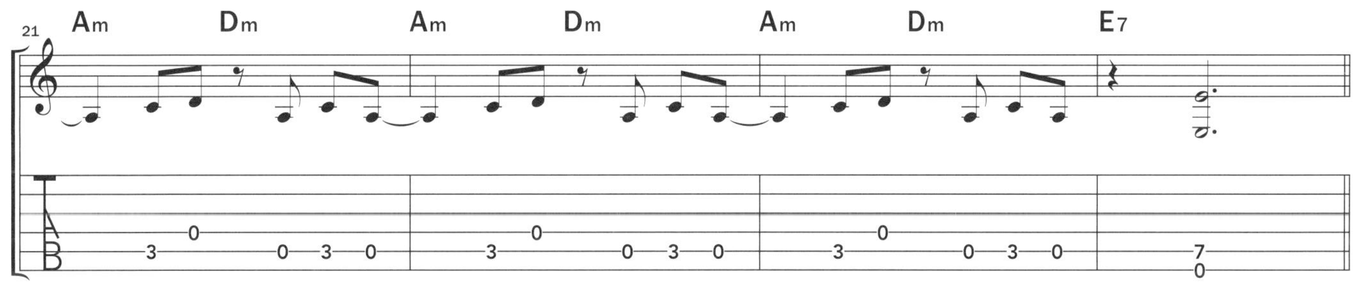

JEFFREY PEPPER RODGERS PHOTO

CLUSTER CHORDS

Think of the opening chord of Neil Young's "Old Man"—a stark minor with a touch of dissonance. Fretted with just two fingers, that chord is a Dm9, and its edgy sound comes from what's on top: two notes, E and F, a half step apart on adjacent strings. You don't need to know any of this theoretically. You just feel the emotion and tension in the harmony, which alternates between that minor ninth and a comforting D major.

That "Old Man" chord is one example of the evocative sounds you can create using chord voicings with notes close to each other—just a half step or whole step apart. Often referred to as cluster chords, these chords may have complicated suffixes like m(add9), add11, or m(♭6), but you don't have to be a jazz player to reach them. You can take advantage of open strings to add these close intervals, often with easy fingerings, and create complex, surprising harmonies that sound particularly great on acoustic guitar.

In this lesson we'll build a vocabulary of cluster chords by adding notes to basic major, minor, and seventh chords, mostly low on the neck. Along the way, we'll check out additional examples based on classic songs by James Taylor, Bob Dylan, Janis Ian, Dave Matthews, and more in which cluster chords are central to the sound.

Add9 Chords

To start, let's focus on cluster chords that add the ninth (aka the second, depending on how the notes are stacked) to major, minor, or seventh chords. First play through the add9 chords in **Example 1**. In all these chords, the ninth is one step below the third. In Cadd9, for instance, the ninth is D (on the second string) and adjacent to the third, E (open first string). The same pattern holds for the add9 voicings of A, G, E, and D. The last Aadd9 shape in the example is the movable version of the Eadd9 shape, and it's a stretch for sure but useful to know (and you can always use part of the shape, such as just the bottom three strings). The cluster in these chords has a soft sound; you can sub an add9 for a regular major for a noticeable but gentle sweetening of the harmony.

A similar set of chords includes the ninth/second but omits the third—so you've got a three-note chord with the root, second, and fifth, known as a sus2, and a close interval between the root and the second. **Example 2** shows common sus2 voicings for D, A, and F. On the Asus2, for instance, there's an A root on the third string next to the second, B.

When you add a ninth to a minor chord, the cluster is tighter—there's just a half step between the ninth and the (minor) third, as in the m(add9) voicings in **Example 3**. In the Em(add9), for instance, the F♯ note on the fourth string rubs against the G note on the third string; the third Am(add9) shape shown is the movable version of this shape (again, a bit of a finger buster, but good to know). The Dm(add9) lacks the fifth and contains only the root (D), ninth (E), and minor third (F).

The minor chord shapes in **Example 4** extend the harmony by adding the ninth to a minor seventh chord. The resulting chords are simply named m9 (the 9, in this case, implies the presence of the flatted seventh).

Don't get too bogged down in all these numbers—just get lost in the rich sound of these chords, and check out a few more famous songs that use them.

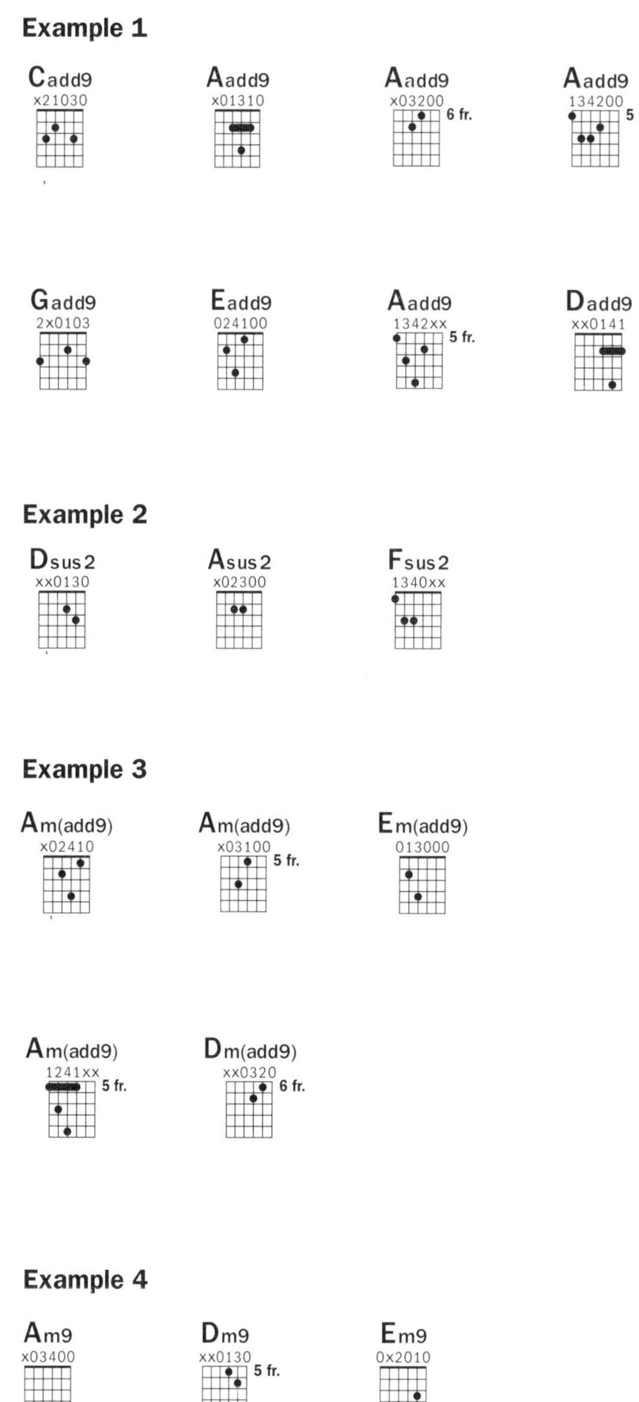

The Em9 is a go-to James Taylor shape, featured, for instance, in the intro to "Something in the Way She Moves." In **Example 5**, alternate between A and Em9 shapes (capoed at the third fret).

Example 6 shows the "Old Man" Dm9–D riff described at the beginning of the lesson.

Example 7 is based on the Police's "Every Breath You Take," a showcase for add9 chords. The original uses A shapes that require some wide stretches. This version of the progression is in the friendlier key of G, and every chord is dressed up with a ninth or second—an essential part of the sound and mood of that song. Use a flatpick and palm muting for a more percussive feel.

Example 5
Capo III

Example 6

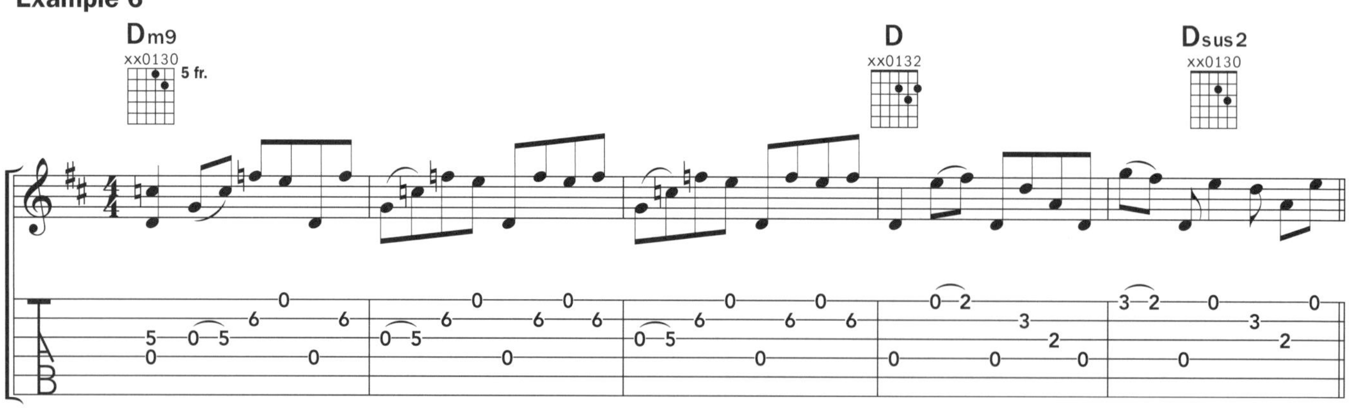

Example 7

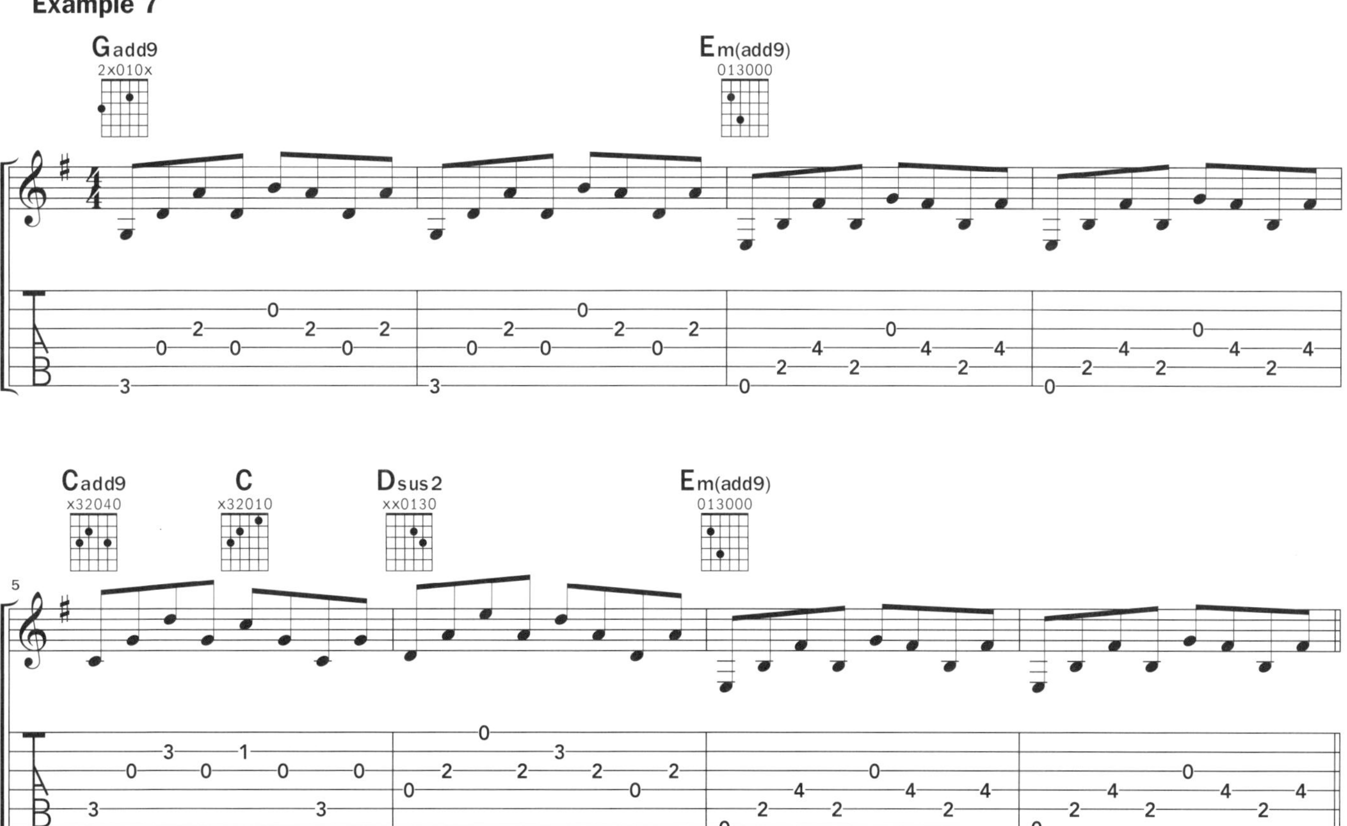

Add4 Chords

Now let's explore a different type of cluster chord that incorporates the fourth (aka the 11th) along with the third. In a major chord, the third and fourth are a half step apart; in a minor chord, the interval is a whole step.

By far the most common of these chords is Dadd4, as in **Example 8**—all you do is slide a C shape up two frets and leave the third string open, and boom, there it is. If you include the open first string, you wind up with Dadd4/9, another sweet-sounding chord.

Example 8

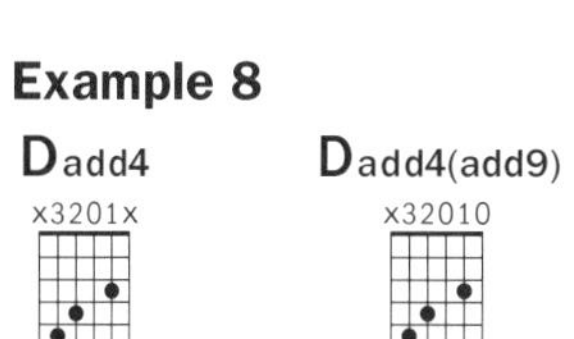

Typically, guitarists use this gussied-up D as the V chord in the key of G—as in, for instance, Bob Dylan's "It Ain't Me, Babe." In **Example 9**, based on the beginning of the verse, go between Dadd4/9 and C twice, and resolve to the G.

You can find great-sounding cluster voicings with the fourth on chords that you may not ordinarily favor—like F♯, where you've got the fourth (B) on the open second string.

Check out the shapes in **Example 10**. Rather than holding down a full barre F♯, leave the second string open for an F♯add11; add in the open first string (the flatted seventh) for an F♯11. The F♯m11 is a nice, easy fingering too, and the Gm11 is a movable version of the same shape that's very handy. In James Taylor's version of "You've Got a Friend," F♯m11 and B7 create an elegant transition between G major and E minor. **Example 11** is based on the intro.

Example 9

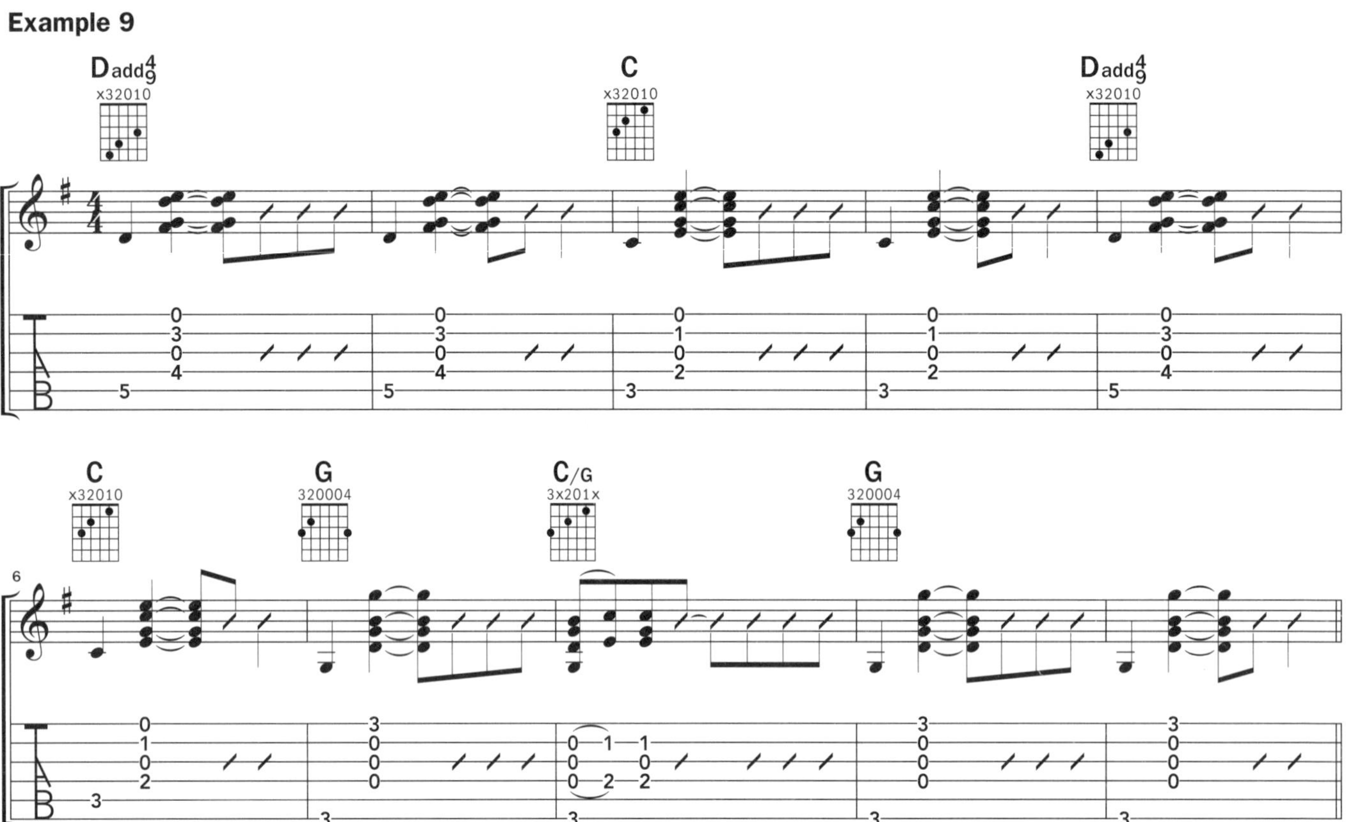

Example 10

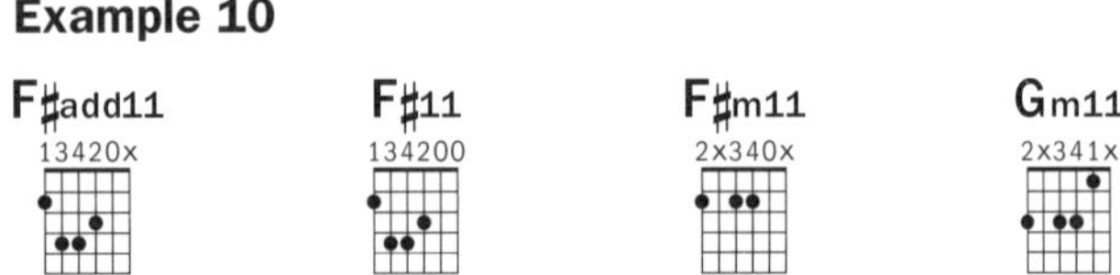

There are a bunch of sweet cluster shapes in the B chord family too, in which the high E string is the fourth and you've got a root on the open second string as well. Check out a few variations for both B major and B minor chords in **Example 12**.

The Badd4 up at the seventh fret is a great alternative to a full barre chord. This voicing includes notes a half step apart, but they are not on adjacent strings; the third (D♯) is on the third string, while the fourth (E) is on the first string, so they are more separated and the dissonance is softer. Combine the seventh-fret Badd4 with voicings of E5, Cm7, and Aadd9 that also leave the top strings open, and you've got the huge-sounding progression in **Example 13**, similar to what Dan Bern uses in "God Said No."

I use the Bm(add11), with the first string open, all the time as a substitute for a regular Bm barre chord. The Bm11—shown three ways in Ex. 12—works nicely in conjunction with E7 for a ii–V change in the key of A, as in **Example 14**.

With the add4 and add11 shapes, try playing the cluster chord for a few beats and then resolving to a regular major or minor.

Major Sevenths

Another group of lovely sounding clusters can be found for major seventh chords. The major seventh is a half step below the root, and you can take advantage of open strings to place those two notes next to each other in the chord, rather than spread apart. Play a set of major seventh chords like this in **Example 15**.

Example 14

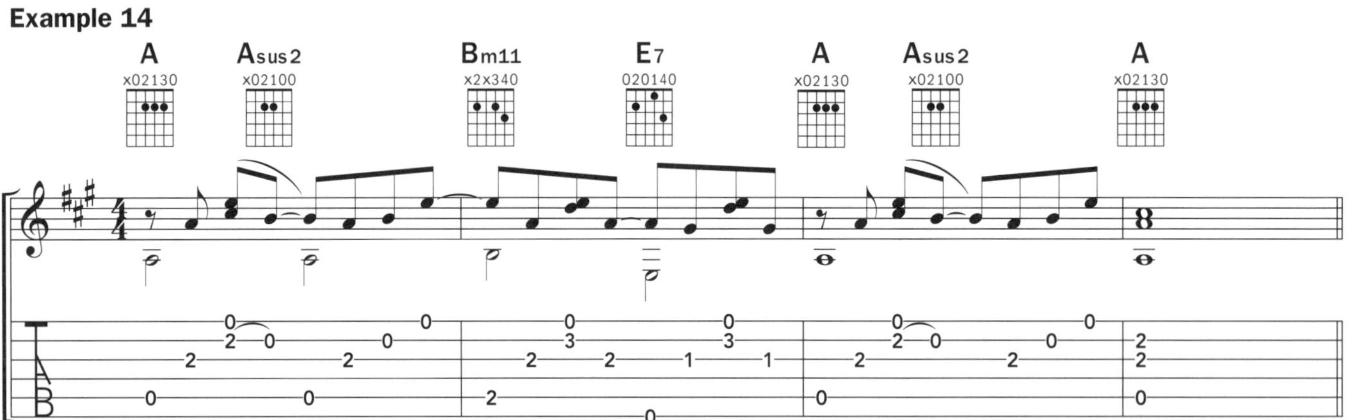

Example 15

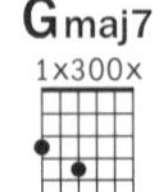

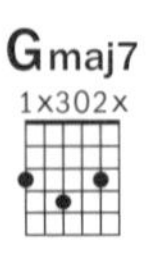

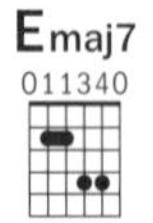

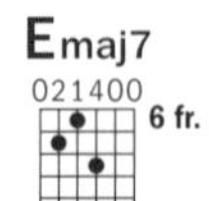

In the Gmaj7 chords, the major seventh (F♯) is on the fourth string, next to the root (G) on the open third string. The second Gmaj7 shape leaves out the third for a more streamlined sound. For the Cmaj7 chords, play the root (C) up the neck against the major seventh (B) on the open second string. For Emaj7, you've got some lush options with lots of open strings—these are just gorgeous chords.

I make use of these major sevenths and other cluster chords in my arrangement of the Grateful Dead's "Eyes of the World" (included in my Homespun video series on Dead songs for acoustic guitar). **Example 16** shows part of the verse rhythm, with Emaj7 up the neck coupled with Aadd9 and Bm(add11) for a gently jazzy sound. Strum with a pick and add a light percussive scratch on beat 2 in the first three measures.

The beautiful bossa nova–inspired accompaniment to Janis Ian's "At Seventeen" includes several cluster chords—maj7 as well as add9. Play the song's main fingerstyle pattern in **Example 17**, using Gadd9, G, Gmaj7, and G6 (capo at the fifth fret to sound in the original key of C).

In other songs, try substituting one of these major seventh cluster chords for a major I or IV chord, to create a gently jazzy sound.

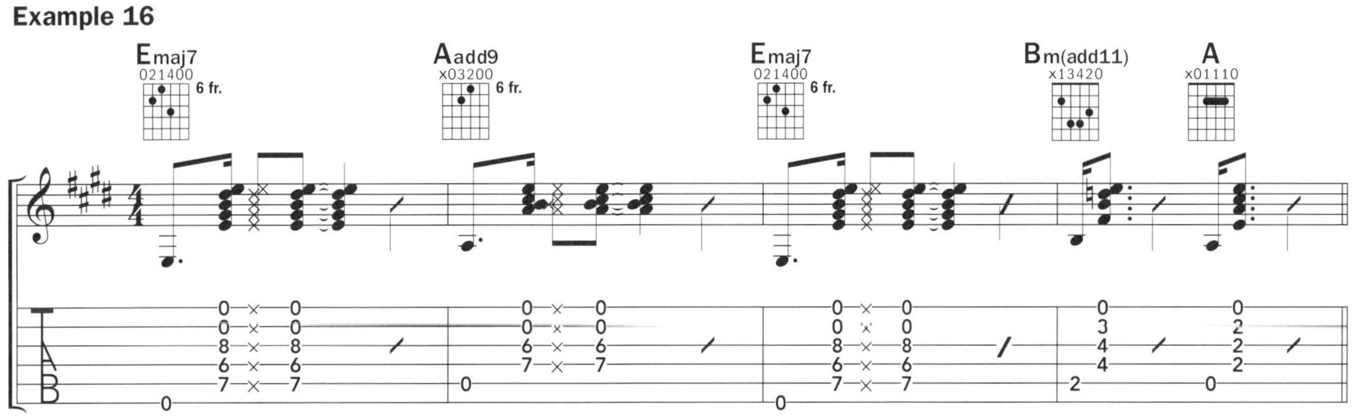

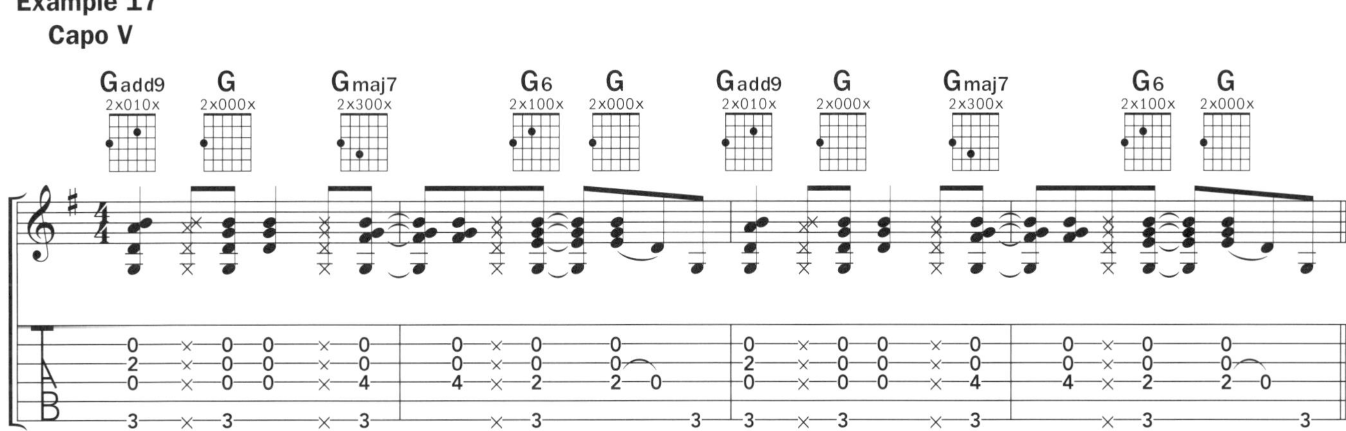

Sixth Chords and More

With further experimentation, you can find many more cluster chords that use other extensions. Here are a few additional sets of chords to try, along with examples of songs that use them.

The chord shapes in **Example 18** add the sixth. In the D6, G6, and B♭6 voicings, the fifth and sixth are a step apart on adjacent strings; in D6, for instance, the fifth is A (third string) and the sixth is B (open second string). All these make nice substitutions for major chords. Try out the D6 in **Example 19**, a guitar rendition of the opening verse accompaniment (played on keyboard on the original record) in the Beatles' "The Fool on the Hill."

The Em13 in Ex. 18, fretted with just one finger, uses a different cluster: the sixth (C♯ on the fifth string) next to the flatted seventh (D on the open fourth string). This chord sounds a bit diffuse on its own—you wouldn't likely want to hang out on it for long. It makes a potent combo with a regular Em, though, as shown in **Example 20**, the main rhythmic figure in my song "Stop, Drop, and Roll." The dissonance of the cluster chord helps create the urgent, unsettled feeling of that song.

If you grab a Bm shape but skip the barre and leave the third string open, you get the mysterious-sounding Bm(♭6) in **Example 21**. Add in the open first string and you've got a Bm11(♭6)—a chord with a complicated name but an easy fingering. Dave Matthews taps into this m♭6 sound in his song "Crush"; he plays in dropped-D tuning, though the tuning isn't needed for the cluster. Try a piece of the verse progression in **Example 22**. The ♭6 cluster chord brings this whole sequence to life.

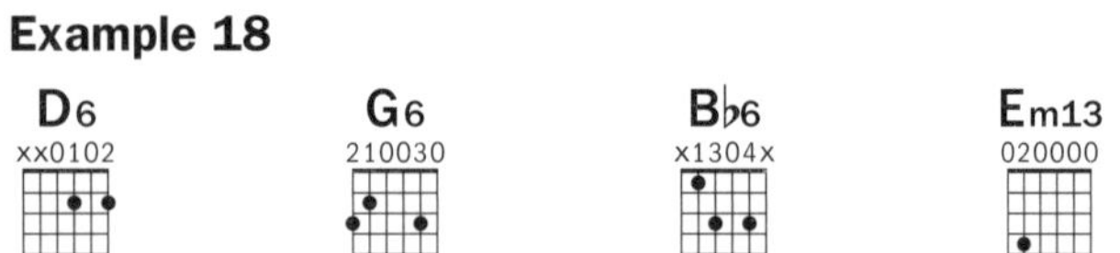

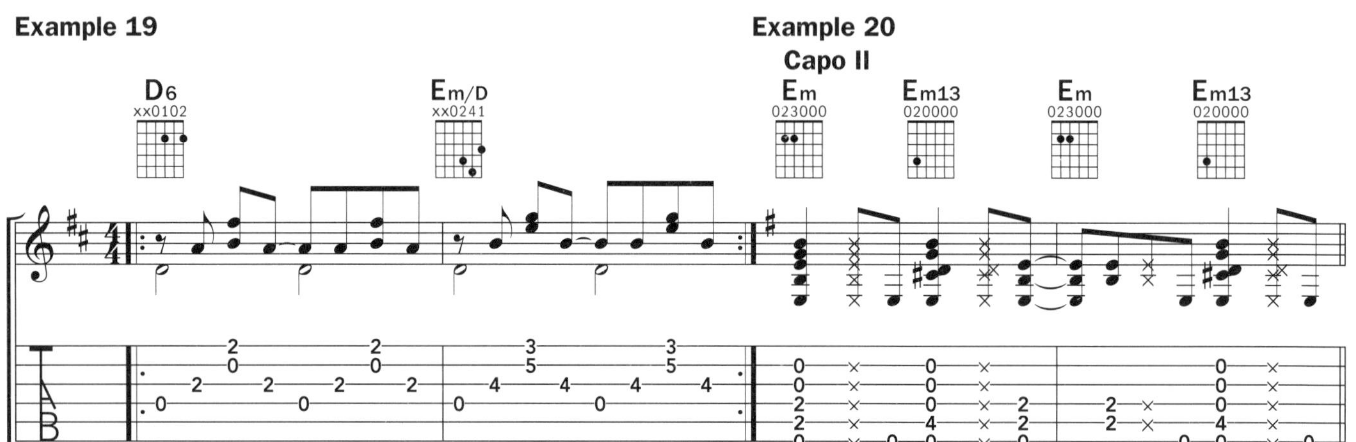

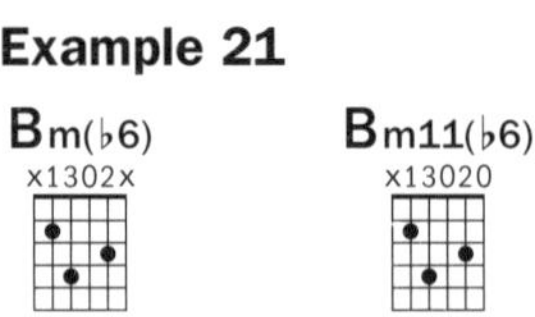

As a final note, alternate tunings open up all kinds of possibilities for cluster chords. I use dropped D all the time and have discovered many cluster voicings in it. **Example 23**, from the instrumental section of my song "Here," takes advantage of having a low D on the sixth string to spotlight the close interval between F♯ on the fourth string and the G on the open third string.

Experiment with Open Strings

As these examples suggest, you can often discover cluster chords just by playing around with fingerings, especially leaving strings open that would usually be fretted. Some of the sounds you find may be too dissonant or strange for your ears. But at other times, you may be surprised to find that introducing clusters and extending the harmony just by one note can transform your guitar part—and maybe lead you to your next song.

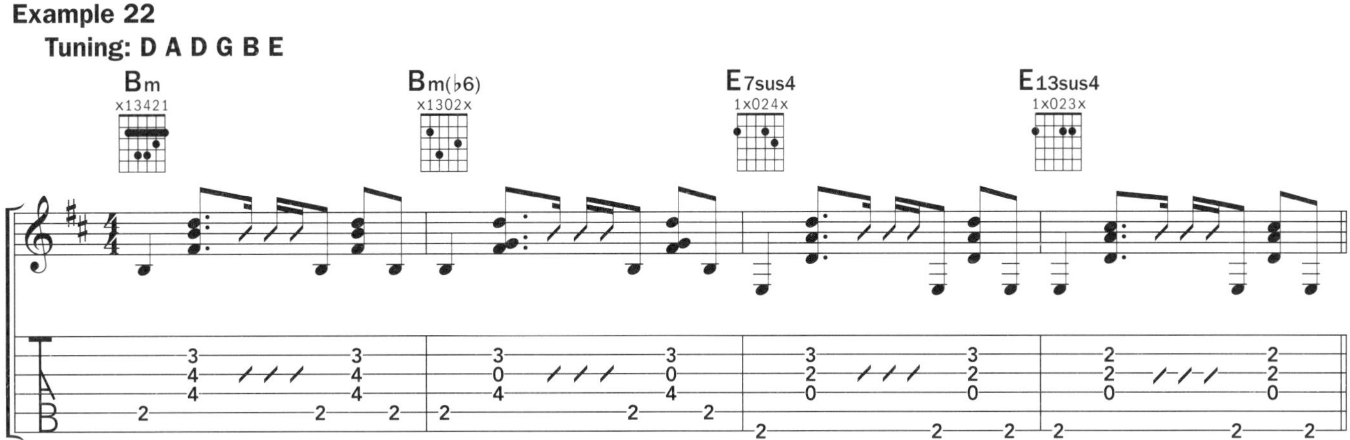

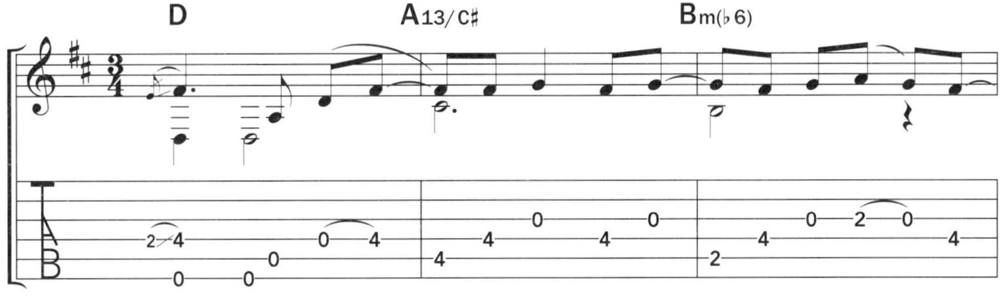

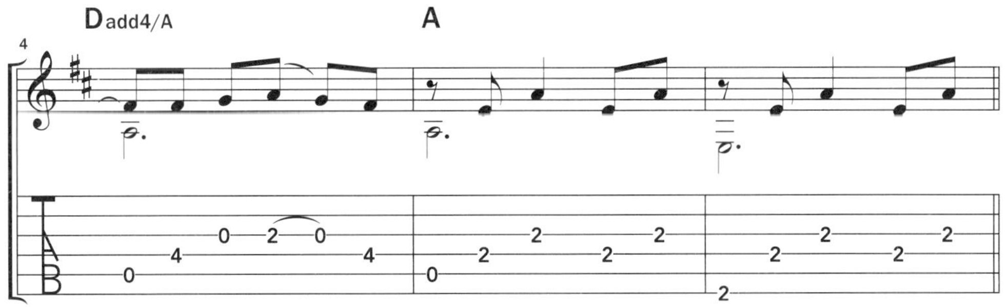

JEFFREY PEPPER RODGERS PHOTO

DOUBLE-DROPPED-D TUNING

If you've ventured into dropped-D tuning on guitar, a great next step into the world of alternate tunings is double dropped D, where you not only lower your sixth string from E to D (as in dropped D) but do the same with your first string. Those two dropped strings open up enticing new possibilities on both the low and high ends of the guitar, while also leaving the four middle strings alone, so much of what you know on the fingerboard in standard tuning still works.

For evidence of the potential of double dropped D, also called D modal by the best-known employer of this tuning, Neil Young, look no further than songs by Led Zeppelin, the Doobie Brothers, Fleetwood Mac, Joni Mitchell, Bob Dylan, Elliott Smith, Michael Hedges, and of course Mr. Young himself. (See "Double-Dropped-D Song Sampler.") As these artists demonstrate, the tuning lends itself to both fingerstyle and flatpick playing.

In this lesson we'll get oriented in double dropped D by looking at common chord shapes, and then we'll check out examples inspired by classic songs.

Detune

First, tune those first and sixth strings down a whole step, so your open string pitches are D A D G B D. In double dropped D you are close to some other common tunings. If you also lower the fifth string a whole step, you'll have open G (D G D G B D); lower the second string a step from double dropped D and you're in DADGAD.

In double dropped D, you've got a few key assets on your open strings. You have D strings in three octaves, unlocking some serious drone potential. You also have a no-fretting D power chord (D–A–D) on the bottom three strings, which means you can also play one-finger power chords on those same strings anywhere on the neck. And you've got a G major chord on the top four open strings.

First, check out the array of D shapes in **Example 1**. Not surprisingly given all the D notes in the tuning, lots of strong D voicings are available. The two-finger D5 is a core shape in double dropped D—it's all roots (D) and fifths (A), with no third, so the chord is neither major nor minor.

Fret the first string as you would in a standard tuning D and you get Dsus2—another chord lacking a third. Moving along the row of chord grids, check out the Dm and D7. Then head up the neck for D major and minor voicings at the sixth/seventh frets and at the tenth/11th. Because of the tuning, you can leave the low strings and the high string open for a lush blend of fretted and open strings.

Now play through some other chords in **Example 2**. G major requires very little fretting. To get a low root, just include the sixth string, fifth fret. As shown, you can hold down both low strings at the fifth fret or just fret the sixth string and mute the fifth string by leaning your fretting finger against it. On the top end, you can leave the first string open or fret the G note at the fifth fret.

Bm is a nice, easy shape with no barre. For C, if you hold the usual shape but include the open first string, you get a sweet-sounding Cadd9. You can also find Cadd9 at the eighth fret; this is a useful shape you can move around the neck to play, as shown, F6 and B♭ as well as other chords.

In **Example 3** you'll find a selection of A chords. The first-string D note is the fourth of an A chord, so you can easily play sparkly cluster voicings that add the fourth to A, A7, Am, and Am7. In an E chord, the first-string D is the flatted seventh, so including the open first string gives you the E7 and Em7 shapes shown (some of these shapes also have a flatted seventh on the open fourth string). The final chord shape, Gm7, is the barre version of the second Em7—a movable shape that's handy to know.

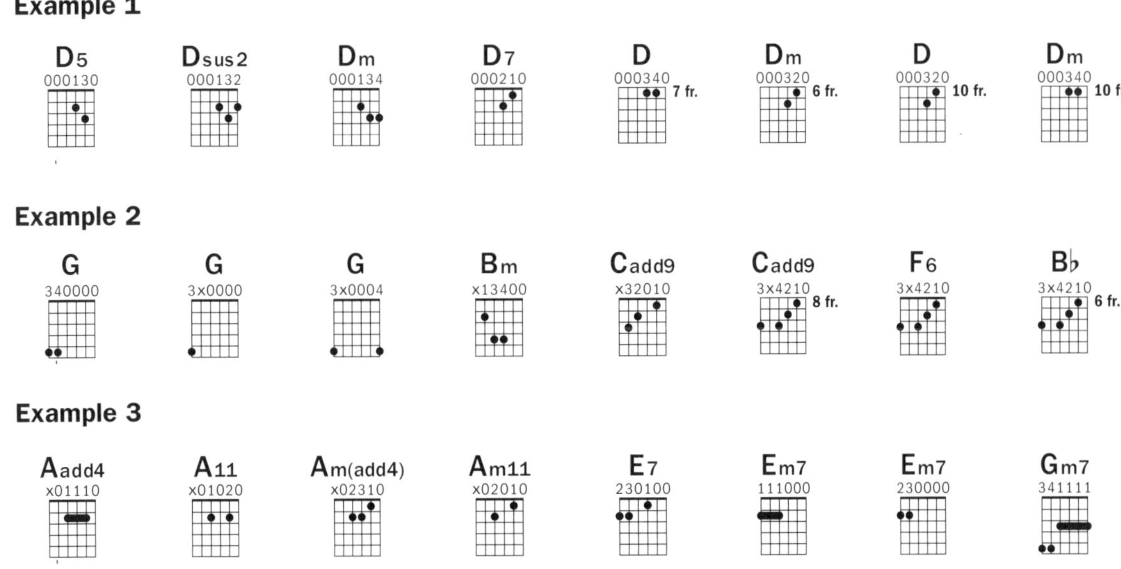

Dig into Drones

Now let's play a few examples inspired by songs that make the most of the big drone sounds of double dropped D.

Bob Dylan's early story song "Ballad of Hollis Brown" chugs along on a D5 for its entire five minutes. Capo at the first fret to be in tune with the track on *The Times They Are A-Changin'*. In **Example 4**, hold the D5 shape with your first and third fingers, and fret the C and F notes on the fifth and fourth strings with your second finger. This simple pattern, with small variations, continues through the whole song.

Another song in double dropped D that's heavy on the drones is Led Zeppelin's "Going to California." Multiple guitars and mandolin fill out the original track, but the foundation is Jimmy Page's double-dropped-D fingerpicking.

Check out the first four bars of **Example 5**: nothing but D notes on four strings in a hypnotic pattern fingerpicked over an alternating bass. Continuing in measure 5, switch to a G at the fifth fret and add a little melody on the top two strings. Notice how seamlessly you can slide up to the D in measure 9 and use the add4 colors. The tuning lends itself beautifully to sus4 and add4 embellishments.

D Modal Moves

No dive into double dropped D would be complete without some Neil Young grooves, so those are the focus of the next series of examples.

Example 6 is based on the main riff in "Ohio." The guitar part uses a D5 that leaves the tonality open, but the vocal melody clearly establishes the key of D minor. Hammer onto the third string of the D5 shape in bars 1 and 3. Mark the changes to F and C mostly with the bass notes. With all three chords, play the open third string as a transition to the next chord.

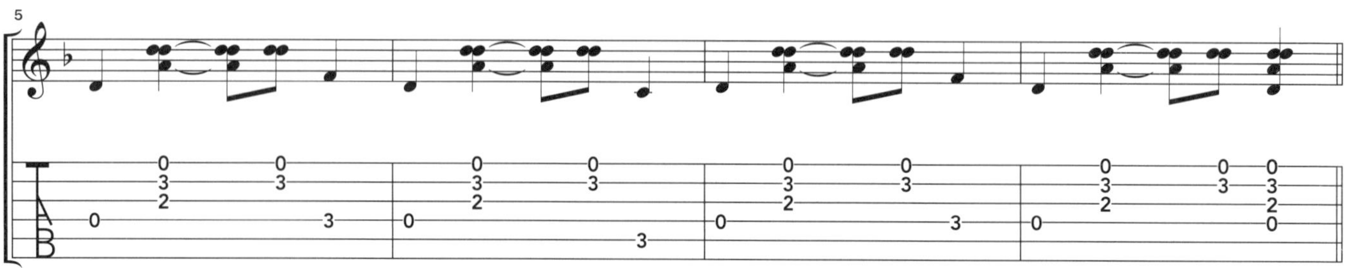

Example 5

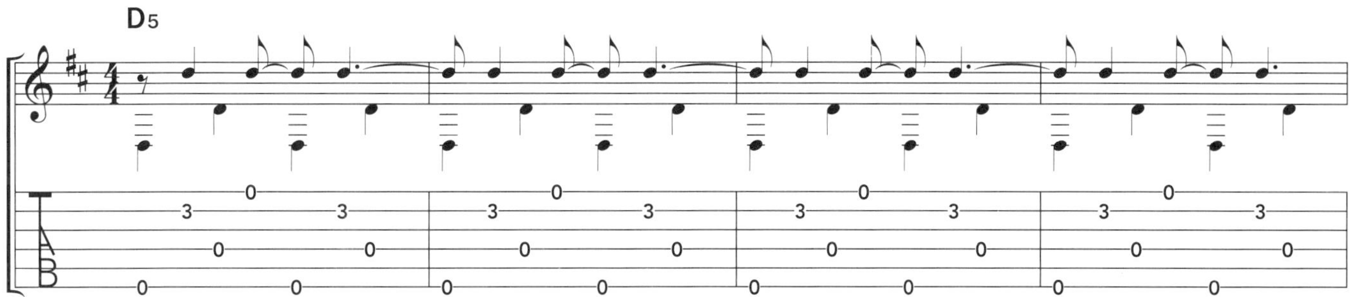

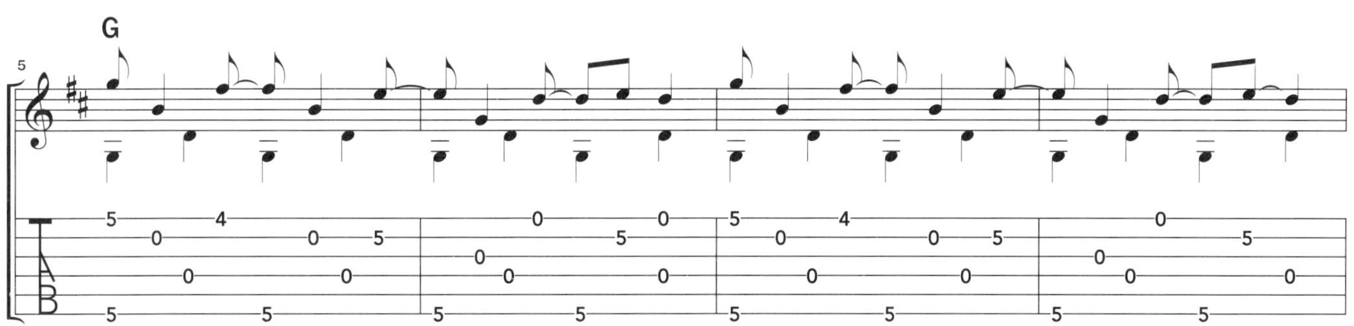

Example 6

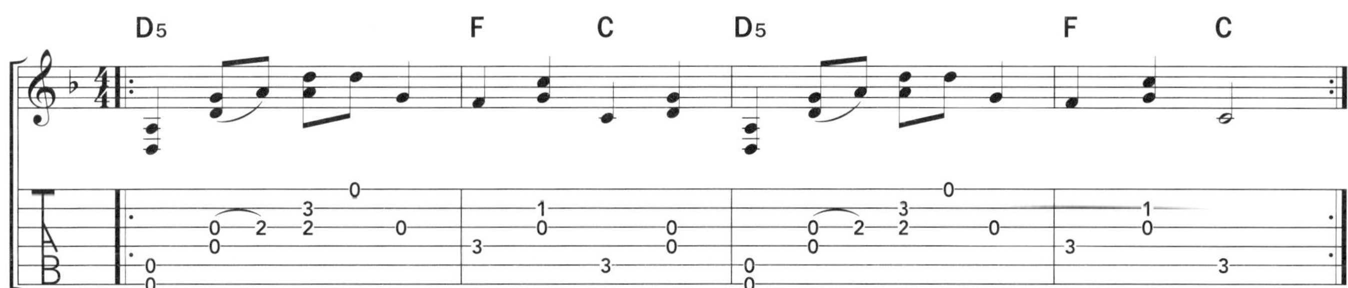

In the chorus of "Ohio," the chords move to Gm7 and Cadd9, as shown in **Example 7**. The dropped first string brings a special flavor to both chords—adding the flatted seventh atop the Gm7 and the ninth to the C.

The next example is inspired by the rocking "Cinnamon Girl." In **Example 8**, start with a slide from C to D chords on the treble strings, then head to the low strings for the answering line in bar 2 that ends with an F to G power chord move. Young typically plays this one on a cranked-up electric, but it has plenty of drive on acoustic guitar as well. In a rocking song like this, play percussively and use palm muting to bring out the drive.

While all the examples so far have been in the key of D, either major or minor, double dropped D can sound great in other keys. A case in point is **Example 9**, based on Young's wistful "One of These Days," in the key of A. On the A chord, the dropped first string contributes the ringing add4. In bar 2, play the same minor seventh shape used in Ex. 7, but moved down a fret for F♯m7. For D, use a Dsus2.

More Classic Patterns

To round out the lesson, let's touch on a few more songs.

One of the quintessential guitar parts in double dropped D comes from the Doobie Brothers—specifically their resident fingerpicker and all-around guitar ace Patrick Simmons. That would be "Black Water," which is built around a Am11-to-D5 figure with a cool bass line.

In **Example 10**, play an A♯-to-B hammer-on on the fifth string leading to the Am11, with that D ringing on the first string. Then play a quick slide up to the F♯ on the sixth string before landing on the D5.

Example 10

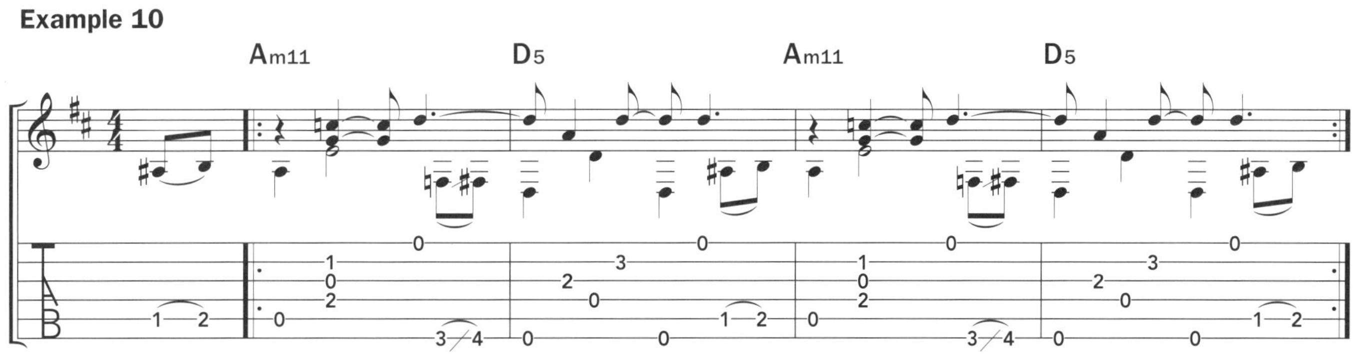

DOUBLE-DROPPED-D SONG SAMPLER

For inspiration, check out these fine examples of double-dropped-D guitar—used to accompany vocals and for a few instrumentals (Nick Drake, Andrew York, Eric Johnson).

Led Zeppelin "Going to California"

Doobie Brothers "Black Water"

Neil Young "Cinnamon Girl"

Bob Dylan "Ballad of Hollis Brown" (capo I)

Joni Mitchell "Free Man in Paris"

Fleetwood Mac "The Chain" (capo II)

Nick Drake "Bryter Layter" (capo III)

Andrew York "Sunburst"

Michael Hedges "Running Blind"

Elliott Smith "Satellite"

Bruce Cockburn "Let the Bad Air Out"

Eric Johnson "Song for George"

The next example comes from my arrangement of Simon and Garfunkel's "The Boxer." For many years I puzzled over how to create the gorgeous cascading guitar intro, played by session guitarist Fred Carter Jr. The secret, I eventually learned, is dropping the first string a step—and then I further discovered that dropping the sixth string as well sweetens the bass lines. (Note that Carter actually used an open tuning with the sixth string raised up to the root, and he also played a baby guitar tuned up a third overall so it sounded in B. I get close to his setup by using double dropped D with a capo at the fourth fret.)

In **Example 11**, get your fretting fingers in place before playing the first two measures: first, second, and fourth fingers on strings 3, 4, and 5, respectively. Then, fingerpick the backward roll, lifting your second finger on the last two beats of bar 2 to play the third string open.

Bar 5 onward shows a sample picking pattern to play under the verse. You're using G shapes, so the low D on the sixth string gives you an alternate bass note under the G chord, as well as a low root when you go to a D chord.

Later in my arrangement (available on YouTube), the tuning facilitates adding an instrumental section, too, based on the pedal steel and piccolo trumpet interlude on the original record.

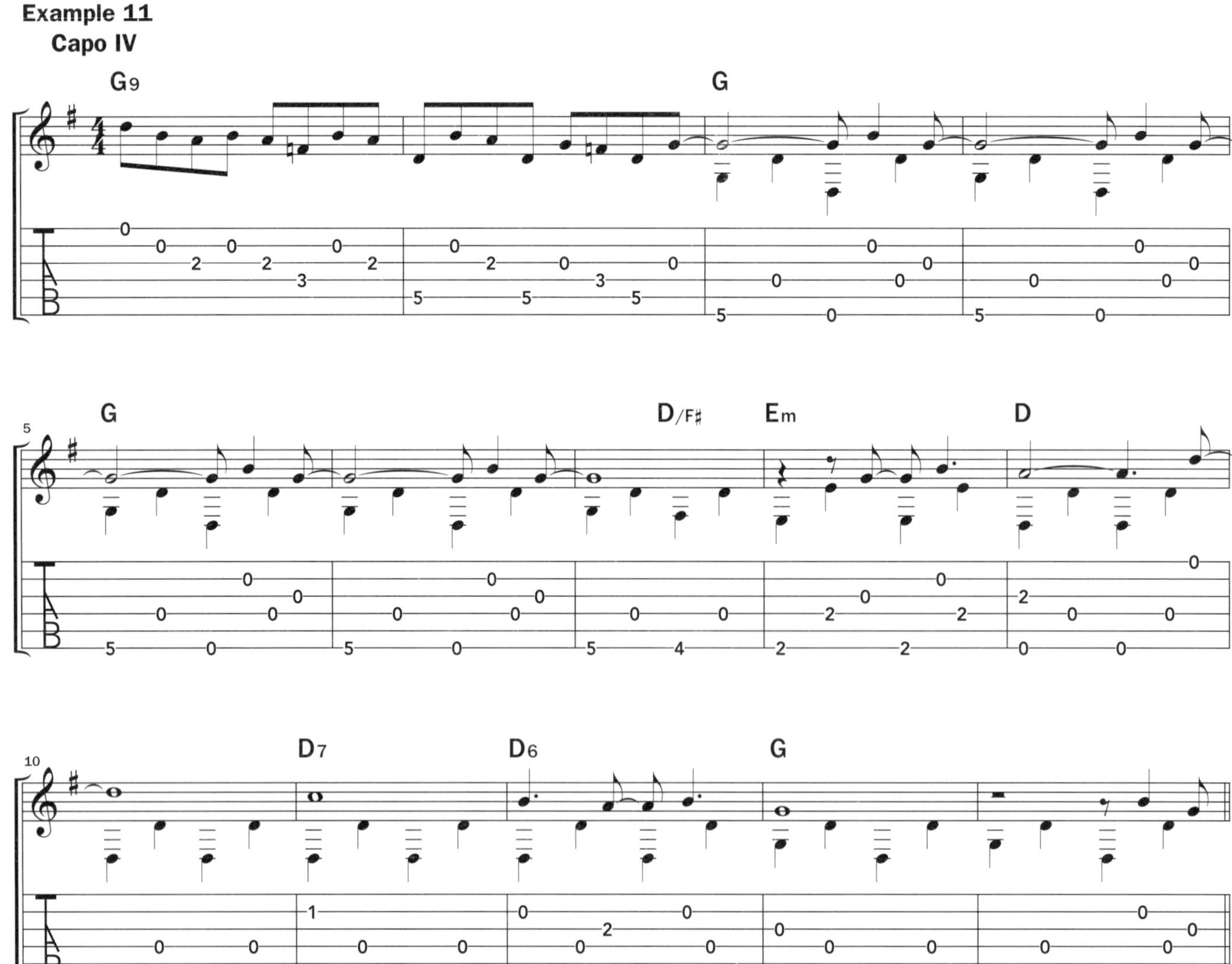

For one final example, Joni Mitchell's "Free Man in Paris" is a great use of double dropped D outside the box of D drones, working both the treble and bass sides of the fingerboard. Try out a sample pattern in **Example 12**. Start with C, D, and F triads on the top strings and then shift to the low strings for C and G on the way to settling into the key of A for the verse. Strum open strings in the transitions between chord shapes.

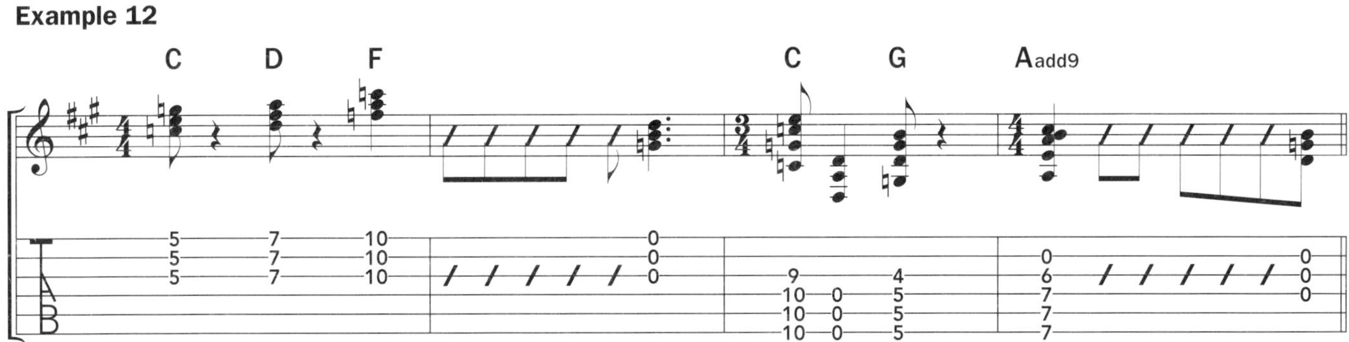

Drop Your Own

Take some of the ideas in these examples and apply them to songs in your own repertoire—or try writing something new in double dropped D. Playing in the key of D is a good place to start, but also consider other keys that might include a D chord, such as G, A, B minor, or E minor. As with any alternate tuning, experiment with leaving strings open that you'd normally be fretting, and see what kinds of sounds you discover.

JEFFREY PEPPER RODGERS PHOTO

EXPLORE THE THREE-STRING CAPO

A partial capo performs a kind of magic trick on your guitar. Fool your friends and baffle your enemies: You sound like you're using an alternate tuning, but you're not!

Partial capos accomplish this sleight of hand by holding down some strings and leaving others untouched—thereby changing the intervals between open strings.

In a lesson in *Beyond Strumming*, I introduced the five-string partial capo, which gives you a setup similar to dropped-D tuning if you place the capo at the second fret covering the top five strings. Now let's explore the three-string capo, designed to hold down strings 3–5 or, flipped around to the other side of the fingerboard, strings 2–4.

The most common use of a three-string capo is on strings 3–5 at the second fret—the capo is grabbing an Esus4 chord shape for you. (Look ma, no fretting!) In that position, the intervals between open strings are the same as in DADGAD tuning up a whole step (E B E A B E). So the capo gives you something like instant DADGAD, while your strings are physically still in standard tuning.

In this lesson, we'll focus mostly on this DADGAD (or Esus) partial capo position—looking at chord shapes and then trying them out in short progressions. For some of the later examples, we will flip the capo around to cover strings 2–4 at the second fret—so it's holding down an A major chord shape.

Unless you want to attempt cutting up a regular capo—not an easy or recommended hack—you'll need a special capo to play these examples. Fortunately three-string capos are readily available and not a big investment: Check out the Shubb C7b, Kyser Short-Cut, D'Addario/Planet Waves Artist DADGAD, G7th Newport three-string model, and others. And the purchase is well worth it for cracking open a whole new candy box of sounds on your guitar.

Essential Shapes

First, put your partial capo in place on strings 3–5 at the second fret. Strum across the open strings to hear the Esus4 chord. You may need to tweak your tuning after adding the capo; I find that a partial capo tends to knock out the tuning a bit.

Now check out the D chord shapes in **Example 1**, starting with the one-finger D5. Note that I'm naming chord shapes in relation to the capo; a D shape sounds as an E. Also note that the top line of these chord grids represents the capo position (second fret). When strings 6, 2, or 1 are open, they actually ring two frets below the capo, at the nut.

Try out the D major, D minor, and D7 shapes, all with lots of open strings. The Dadd4 is a sweet cluster voicing with the third and fourth of the chord next to each other.

Play some G voicings in **Example 2**. You'll notice that the first G shape looks and sounds just like you're in standard tuning—because you are in standard tuning! In the second G shape, leave the first string open. Then open up the second string, too, for a Gadd9. As shown, you can also play a Gadd9 by using the third-fret barre chord shape but leaving the top strings open; the example shows variations fretted with four, three, and two fingers. Finally, check out the Gm shape that's far gentler on the fingers than the usual six-string barre.

Example 3 offers a selection of A major and minor shapes enriched with sus4, add4, and 11 extensions on the open first and second strings. In the last few A shapes, move up the neck while still using open strings on top.

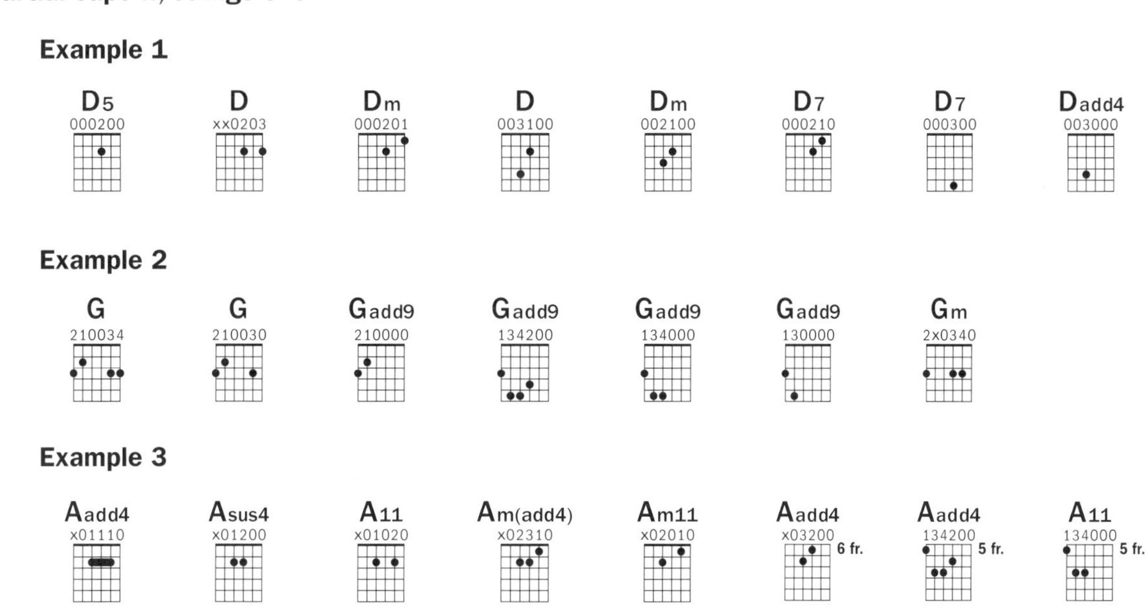

In **Example 4**, play through more chord shapes, starting with a Cadd9 and C9. The E chords present a wrinkle: if you want a low root, you have to fret the sixth string alongside the capo. To accomplish that, you may need to scoot your capo a little further from the second fret (toward the nut) than you would normally place it; look for a sweet spot just far enough from the fret that your index finger can slip in to fret the sixth string, but not so far that it causes the capoed strings to buzz or sound dull. Fretting beside the capo like this may feel awkward at first but gets more comfortable with practice.

Finally, play the Bm7, F6, and Bbmaj7 shapes, all with sparkly open strings on top.

Bear in mind that you can transpose all these chord shapes (and the examples that follow) with a regular capo: just use a regular capo plus a partial capo two frets higher. If you put a regular capo at, say, the third fret, and the partial capo at the fifth fret, your D shapes sound in the key of G.

Instant DADGAD

Now let's dig into some short progressions and riffs with the partial capo. First off, play **Example 5**, a simple I–IV–V–I in the key of D. Sounds familiar, right? You're fretting all the notes on strings 6, 2, and 1, so you get a straight-up standard tuning sound.

Things start to get interesting when you do incorporate more open strings, as in **Example 6**, based on the same progression. Start with the one-finger Dadd4 and play Gadd9, and Aadd4—all voicings that add harmonic color—and end on a D5.

As with DADGAD and other alternate tunings, this partial capo setup lends itself to playing melodic riffs over open string drones. A case in point is **Example 7**, which was my first eureka discovery with the three-string partial capo. This jangly bit of chord melody is an adaptation of George Harrison's electric guitar riff in "Nowhere Man," and it inspired me to arrange the whole song, guitar solo and all, with the partial capo.

The similarity between this three-string capo position and DADGAD means that in many cases you can translate easily between them. I have done that with a number of guitar arrangements. For instance, my DADGAD take

Example 4

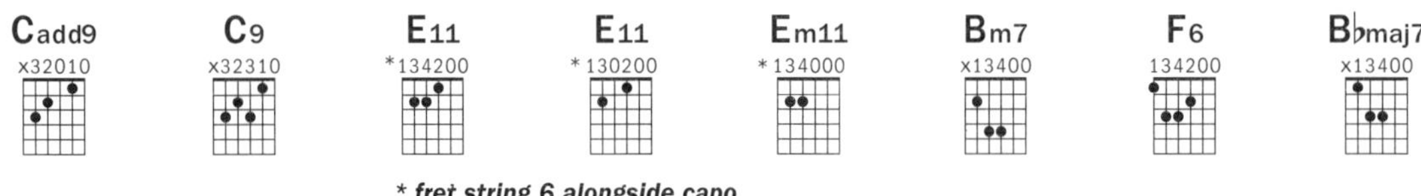

Partial capo II, strings 3–5

Example 5

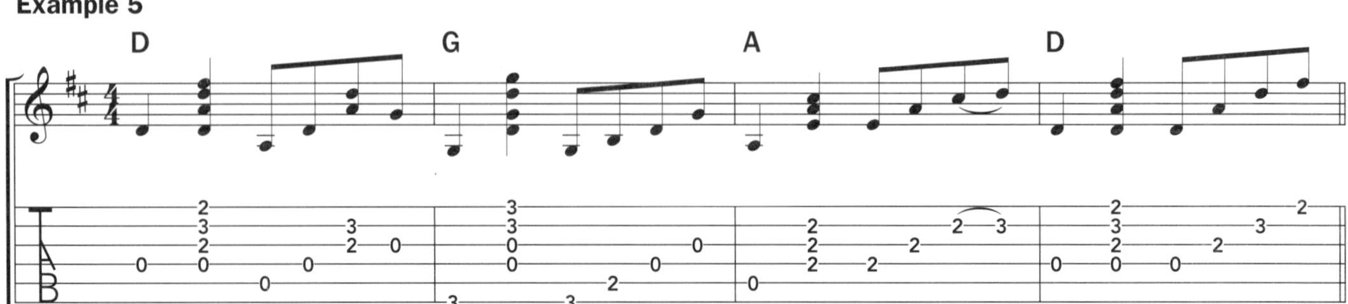

on Pink Floyd's "Wish You Were Here" (published in the book *DADGAD Guitar Essentials*) originated on a three-string capo. In my Homespun video series on Grateful Dead songs for acoustic guitar, I taught "Cassidy" and "Bird Song" in DADGAD but also perform those arrangements with the three-string capo.

Check out a little piece of "Bird Song" in **Example 8**. Play the signature riff on the fourth and fifth strings and use open strings below and above to maintain a D drone. As you play the example, be aware of the meter change from 4/4 to 2/4 in the fourth bar.

Fretting at Zero

Now it's time to tackle some examples that require fretting strings alongside the capo.

With an additional nod to George Harrison, the progression from "My Sweet Lord" works nicely with the three-string capo. In **Example 9**, start off with an Em11 in which you're fretting the sixth string next to the capo. Switch to an Aadd4, which uses the familiar A shape but includes the fourth because of the uncapoed top string. With the Aadd4, as well as the Bm7 and F♯dim7 in subsequent measures, change chords before the downbeat—on the last *and* of the previous measure.

The D5 and Bm7 take advantage of partial-capo-enabled open strings, but the F♯dim7 is just as it would be in standard tuning.

My own song "What I Never Said," built around a drone-heavy guitar part with a three-string capo, also uses an Em with the bass note fretted next to the capo. (On the album track, my guitar is tuned down a whole step to D, but in the video accompanying this lesson I'm at standard pitch.) In **Example 10,** start with a Gadd9 at the third fret, move the same shape down a fret for an F♯m(♭6/♭9) and then down again for an Em11, before landing on a D5.

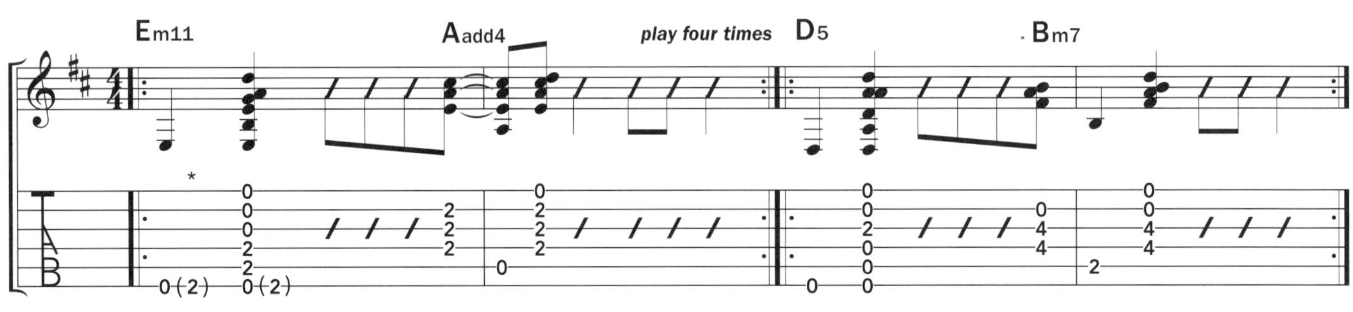

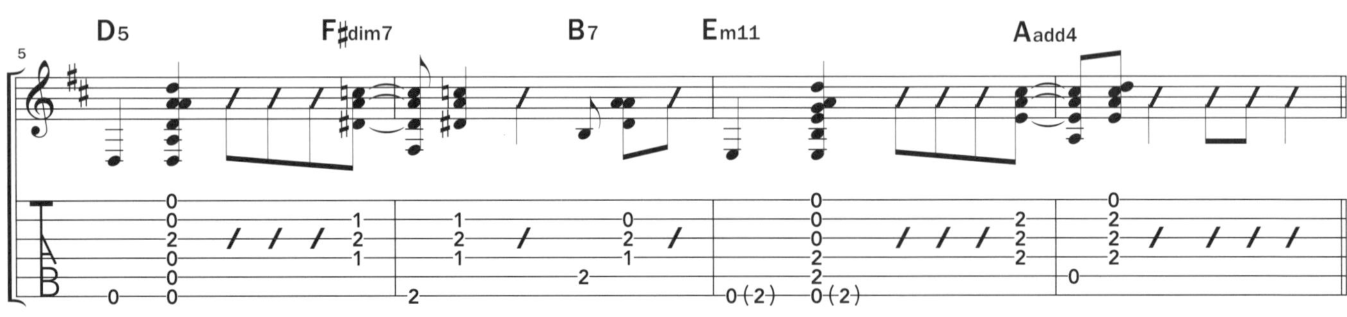

Example 10

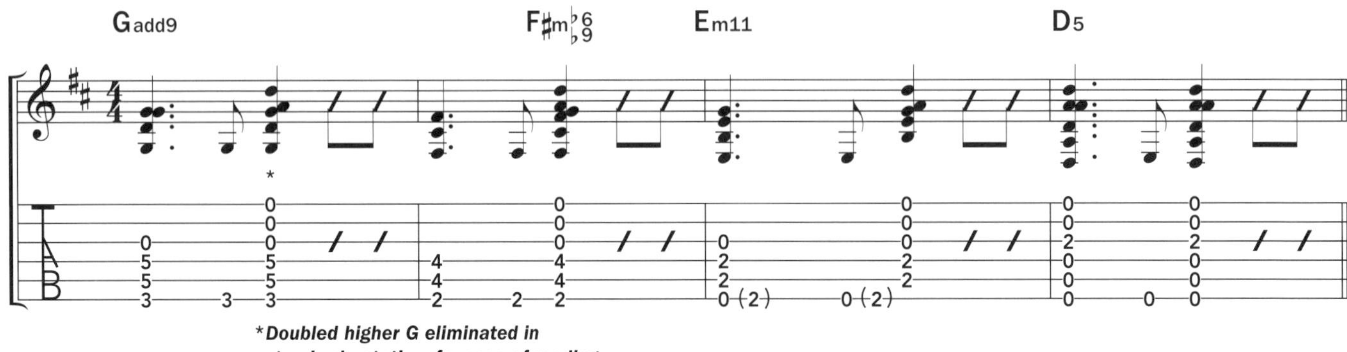

You also may want to play notes on the top string(s) beside the capo. **Example 11**, based on Stephen Foster's "Hard Times," places the melody on the first string. Start on the open first string, and where you see "0 (2)" in tab, fret alongside the capo. Because the capo is on the bass side of the neck, you have easy access to fretting this note. Play this example fingerstyle, and let the open strings ring as long as possible for a chiming alternate-tuning-style sound.

The A Position

Now flip your capo around to the other side of the neck, so it covers strings 2–4 at the second fret. Strum across the strings, and you've got an A major chord. The open string pitches are now E A E A C♯ E, which is the same as in open G tuning (D G D G B D) up a whole step.

This capo position offers a new set of possibilities. First check out a few chord shapes in **Example 12**. Again, I'm naming chords in relation to the capo position, so a G sounds as an A. The first G shape is all open strings—no fretting. You can, however, fret the top and/or bottom strings if you like, as in the next two shapes.

The G7 shape is similar to what you could use in the DADGAD partial capo position, except now you've got a root available on the open fifth string. The Em shape is the same as the one used in Ex. 9 and 10 for Em11; with this capo position, the resulting chord is an Em7. Next, try the Cadd9/G and slide up two frets for Dadd4/G. The latter chord could also function as a Gmaj7. Finally, play a D/F♯ with the same fingering you might use in standard tuning with no capo, except mute the fifth string (lean your ring finger against it) and leave the first string open.

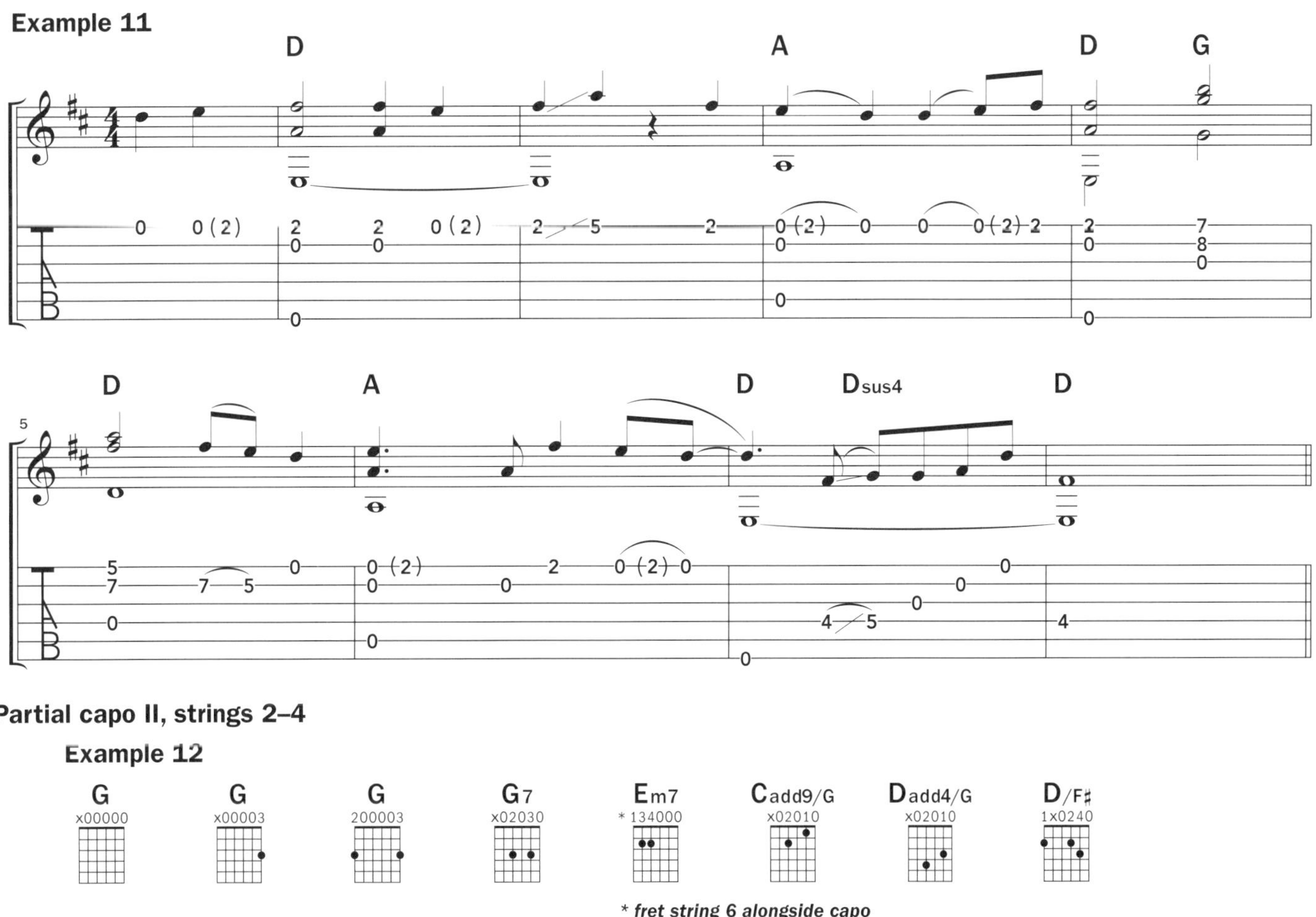

One song that uses this partial capo position is Dan Bern's "Jerusalem," which is the basis for **Example 13**. The sliding G riff in the first two measures may look familiar from standard tuning. The difference here is, because of the capo, you have chord tones available on the open fifth and first strings. You don't actually have to fret the sixth string because you've already got that note on the fifth string, but using both gives you a big, full bass.

Starting in bar 3 of Ex. 13, play a descending G–D/F♯–Em sequence. You can (as Bern often does) leave out the sixth string on the Em to simplify the fingering.

My own song "Fly," which incorporates the fiddle tune "Sally Goodin," takes advantage of the partial capo for flatpicking a melody over my own rhythm. (My original studio recording does not use a partial capo, but the later release on the album *Live and Listening* is played this way, with an extended improv.) Try a piece of the "Fly" guitar part in **Example 14**, based on the A section of "Sally Goodin." Let the open fifth string bass note ring throughout. Play the melody on the third and fourth strings, and add some high drone notes on the upper strings—an effect akin to a banjo's fifth string.

Further Adventures

All of these examples are just a taste of what you can do with a three-string capo. You can of course find many more chord shapes and try other keys, and you can also move the capo to other positions.

Example 15 shows one sample of what you might find moving the three-string capo up the neck. Place the capo on strings 3–5 at the fourth fret, where a C shape sounds as an E. Try this walk-down sequence reminiscent of "Mr. Bojangles," with a low root on the uncapoed sixth string and ringing open strings on top.

If you really want to enter the twilight zone, use a partial capo in conjunction with an alternate tuning.

Beware: It's a slippery slope...but a great ride.

Example 13

G Cadd9/G Dadd4/G Cadd9/G G D/F♯

Em7 Cadd9 G C/G G

*Play actual fret 2

Example 14

Example 15

Partial capo IV, strings 3–5

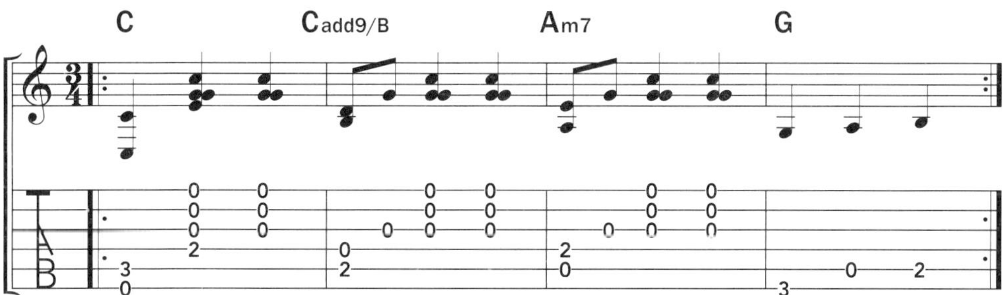

About the Author

Jeffrey Pepper Rodgers has combined his twin passions for words and music into a multifaceted career as a musician, author, and teacher.

A grand prize winner of the John Lennon Songwriting Contest, he plays kinetic folk rock, combining vivid imagery and storytelling with masterful band-in-a-box guitar playing. He performs solo, with the duo Pepper and Sassafras, and with a full acoustic band, and has released five albums of original songs.

He also leads Dead to the Core, a collective of singer-songwriters and acoustic musicians celebrating the Grateful Dead, and created a best-selling video series for Homespun Music Instruction teaching his acoustic arrangements of classic Dead songs.

Rodgers is the founding editor of *Acoustic Guitar* magazine and author of *The Complete Singer-Songwriter*, the multimedia guide *Beyond Strumming*, and the Homespun video *How to Learn Guitar Parts from Recordings*.

A "renowned guitar teacher" (*Boston Globe*), Rodgers has been a staff instructor at Ashokan Acoustic Guitar Camp and Lamb's Retreat for Songwriters, and for over a decade he has taught courses on songwriting and creative nonfiction writing at Syracuse University.

JEFFREY PEPPER RODGERS PHOTO